T0153014

Florida

BY THEME
DAY TRIPS

Mike Miller

Adventure Publications
Cambridge, Minnesota

Dedication

To Yadira Cepero, for being my support and inspiration.

Acknowledgments

I would like to thank Linda, Suzy, Jim, Lee, Cherie, Jean, Robin, and other friends and family for all the miles they wandered around Florida with me discovering new places and things to do.

Safety Note: Florida is home to a variety of potentially dangerous animals, including alligators, sharks, and venomous snakes, as well as natural hazards, such as rip tides. Always heed posted safety warnings, take common-sense safety precautions, and remain aware of your surroundings. You are responsible for your own safety.

Cover and book design by Jonathan Norberg

Front cover photo: Southernmost Point in Florida (photographed by Michael Kaercher/Shutterstock.com)

Back cover photo: Brown Pelican on airboat (photographed by pisaphotography/Shutterstock.com)

All photos by Shutterstock, except pg. 128 by rusty_clark/flickr.com

10 9 8 7 6

Florida Day Trips by Theme
Copyright © 2020 by Michael "Mike" Miller
Published by Adventure Publications
An imprint of AdventureKEEN
310 Garfield Street South
Cambridge, Minnesota 55008
(800) 678-7006
adventurepublications.net
All rights reserved
Printed in China
ISBN 978-1-59193-913-9 (pbk.), ISBN 978-1-59193-914-6 (ebook)

Please note that prices fluctuate in the course of time and that travel information changes under the impact of many factors that influence the travel industry. We therefore suggest that you call ahead for confirmation when making your travel plans. Every effort has been made to ensure the accuracy of information throughout this book, and the contents of this publication are believed to be correct at the time of printing. Nevertheless, the publishers cannot accept responsibility for errors or omissions, for changes in details given in this guide, or for the consequences of any reliance on the information provided by the same. Assessments of attractions and so forth are based upon the author's own experiences; therefore, descriptions given in this guide necessarily contain an element of subjective opinion, which may not reflect the publisher's opinion or dictate a reader's own experience on another occasion.

Table of Contents

Kayaking among the mangroves (photographed by Beth Swanson/Shutterstock)

FLORIDA'S YEAR-ROUND temperate to tropical climate makes it a perfect place for outdoor adventure. The state is bordered by 8,400 miles of saltwater coast, and its interior is bejeweled by more than 30,000 lakes and thousands of miles of rivers and streams. Florida has an extensive state park system, along with national parks, local parks, and bike trails. There are limitless places for boating, fishing, or just plain beachcombing and shell hunting. Florida is made for enjoying the outdoors.

OUTDOOR ADVENTURES

4, 6 Various locations

1 Amelia Island Horseback Riding

4600 Peters Point Road, Amelia Island, Florida 32034; 904-753-1701
ameliaislandhorsebackriding.com

If you've ever dreamed of galloping through foamy surf on a fast horse, this adventure is for you. Debbie Manser has been operating this unique attraction for more than 25 years. You call (or book online) and arrange to meet at Peters Point Beachfront Park in Fernandina Beach, and she trailers the horses in from their stable close to Amelia Island. Once you start riding on the beach, you will do so for 1 hour. Manser can accommodate two to four riders at a time, and with advance notice can handle up to six.

2 Babcock Ranch Eco Tours

8502 FL 31, Punta Gorda, Florida 33982; 800-500-5583
babcockranchecotours.com

Dating to the 1800s, Babcock is among the oldest ranches in Florida's long history of cattle ranching. Encompassing a working cattle ranch with over 55,000 acres of pastureland, it is typical of what Old Florida was all about. On their 90-minute Swamp Buggy Tour, you will traverse Florida ecosystems, seeing the tough bulls and cows known as Cracker cattle that are unique to Florida and possibly catching a glimpse of an endangered Florida panther in its wild home.

3 Bob's River Place

2878 County Road 430, Branford, Florida 32008; 352-542-7363
bobsriverplace.com

A gentleman named Bob Hawkins built this popular tourist attraction on the Suwannee River near Branford. In the early 1970s he built his house on a bluff overlooking the river. The venture started with a tree house and swing that Bob built for his children. He wanted the kids to experience the fun of an old-fashioned swimming hole like he had enjoyed as a kid. Over the years he added waterslides, rope swings, docks, picnic shelters, and ladders so you can jump into the river from a tree.

4 Florida Fish Camps

florida-backroads-travel.com/florida-fish-camps.html

Florida's fish camps provide a glimpse into what the state was like before the massive development that's taken place in recent years. With thousands of miles of coastline and numerous lakes and rivers, fish camps offer boat rentals, fishing gear, and in some cases, overnight lodging. Some of them also provide catch-and-release experiences for the kids.

5 Ginnie Springs Outdoors

5000 NE 60th Ave., High Springs, Florida 32643; 386-454-7188
ginniespringsoutdoors.com

Ginnie Springs Outdoors is a privately owned park that offers a variety of outdoor activities. You can scuba dive, snorkel, camp, go canoeing and kayaking, and enjoy the 200-acre natural Florida setting. There are 129 full-service campsites on the property, along with picnic tables, grills, and bathrooms to serve the campsites. The water in the springs is crystal clear and even received praise from Jacques Cousteau, the father of scuba.

6 Golfing

pga.com/golf-courses/details/fl

With its year-round good climate, Florida is a golfer's paradise. There are courses ranging from small public facilities to tournament-quality private clubs. No matter where in Florida's 67 counties you find yourself, there is sure to be a golf course nearby.

7 Ichetucknee Inner Tube Trip

Ichetucknee Springs State Park, 12087 SW US 27, Fort White, Florida 32038; 386-497-4690
floridastateparks.org/park/ichetucknee-springs

Floating down the Ichetucknee River is a Florida tradition that spans many generations. The crystal-clear river flows 6 miles through shady natural hammocks and wetlands before it reaches the Santa Fe River. There are several private concessions, in addition to the public state park, where inner tubes can be rented. The tubing season is from Memorial Day weekend to Labor Day weekend.

12 Various locations

8 Kayaking at Topsail Hill Preserve State Park

7525 W. County Highway 30A, Santa Rosa Beach, Florida 32459; 850-267-8330
floridastateparks.org/park/topsail-hill

Topsail Hill is one of Florida's natural treasures. It includes miles of white sand beaches on the Gulf of Mexico with dunes more than 25 feet high. It also features three rare coastal dune lakes. Visitors can canoe, kayak, or paddleboard on the Gulf. Personal watercraft can be rented at the park.

9 Scalloping in the Gulf of Mexico

Florida Fish and Wildlife Conservation Commission, 620 S. Meridian St., Tallahassee, Florida 32399; 850-488-4676
myfwc.com/fishing/saltwater/recreational/bay-scallops

Scalloping season is usually July–September. During season, thousands of people gather along the Gulf Coast from south of Steinhatchee up to the Carrabelle area. Their fishing equipment consists of snorkel gear and buckets. A saltwater fishing license is required to harvest the tasty little critters unless you wade into the shallow waters and feel for the animals with your feet and hands without using a mask or snorkel.

10 Sea Turtles Nesting

Sea Turtle Preservation Society, 111 S. Miramar Ave., Indialantic, Florida 32903; 321-676-1701
seaturtlespacecoast.org

Florida has an abundant supply of beautiful sand beaches, and sea turtle nesting season is every year from May to October. The mother turtles crawl up the beach to the dune line, dig holes in the sand, and lay their eggs. Some experts say that sea turtles make 40,000–84,000 nests each year on Florida beaches. A favorite place to observe this nesting activity is on Florida's east coast. The Sea Turtle Preservation Society is located near the center of this stretch, in Indialantic near Melbourne Beach. When observing sea turtles, never disturb a nest or use flash photography or shine lights on nests.

11 Withlacoochee State Trail

3100 S. Old Floral City Road, Inverness, Florida 34450; 352-726-0315
floridastateparks.org/trail/withlacoochee

The Withlacoochee State Trail is a 46-mile-long path follows an abandoned railroad route that is roughly parallel to the nearby Withlacoochee River. The path is now paved and is a great location to hike, bike (no motors), and skate. It's mostly flat so even geezers and out-of-shape people can enjoy it. You can start the path at either end (north or south) or at one of the towns or villages along the route. There are stores along the route and restrooms too. There is also a bike repair and rental shop in Floral City.

12 Zip Lines

ziplinerider.com/florida_ziplines.html

Zip-lining is another year-round outdoor activity made possible by Florida's moderate climate. Zip lines are found in many adventure courses and theme parks, and in Florida a large number of them are located in natural settings where you can soar through the treetops. There are even places where you can fly safely above alligators and other wildlife. Some of the zip lines are for beginners, and others involve challenging obstacle courses.

Miccosukee Tribal Art (photographed by Birute Vijeikiene/Shutterstock)

THERE WERE MANY NATIVE AMERICAN TRIBES living in Florida before the Spanish arrived in the 1500s. Most of them disappeared within 200 years, either dying of European diseases or after being enslaved in the Caribbean. The Seminoles emerged in the 1700s from a combination of various tribes who settled in Florida. The dominant tribe was the northern Muscogee Creeks from Georgia and Alabama. By 1842 most Seminoles had been forcibly relocated to reservations west of the Mississippi River. The remaining population fought the third of three wars against the United States. In the 20th century, the Miccosukee became its own recognized tribe.

SEMINOLE INDIAN CULTURE

4 Various locations

1 Ah-Tah-Thi-Ki Museum

Big Cypress Seminole Indian Reservation, 34725 W. Boundary Road, Clewiston, Florida 33440; 877-902-1113
ahtahthiki.com

This museum in the heart of the Big Cypress Seminole Indian Reservation has a collection of more than 180,000 artifacts and a variety of on-site artisans. You will learn about the Seminole people and their rich historical and cultural ties to the state of Florida and the southeastern United States. The museum grounds include a 1-mile raised boardwalk that meanders through a 60-acre cypress dome typical of the Everglades. You will also see a Seminole village and ceremonial grounds.

2 Billie Swamp Safari

30000 Gator Tail Trail, Clewiston, Florida 33440; 863-983-6101
billieswamp.com

Billie Swamp Safari, also on the Big Cypress Seminole Indian Reservation, features tours and attractions that will teach you about Seminole culture. Among the experiences is a 55-minute swamp buggy ecotour through the natural settings of the Everglades. Or you can take an airboat ride, where you will see fish, snakes, turtles, and alligators. The Seminoles also put on a snake show, and various animal exhibits feature birds and reptiles.

3 Dade Battlefield Historic State Park

7200 Battlefield Pkwy., Bushnell, Florida 33513; 352-793-4781
floridastateparks.org/park/dade-battlefield

This park was established in 1921 to preserve and commemorate the site of Dade's Battle of 1835, which precipitated the longest and costliest Indian war in American history. An annual battle reenactment takes place here in January, and a small museum at the visitor center features exhibits such as an award-winning, 12-minute video about the historic battle. The park has beautiful grounds, picnic pavilions, and hiking trails.

4 | Seminole Wars Heritage Trail

Numerous locations across the state
dos.myflorida.com/historical/preservation/heritage-trails/seminole-wars-heritage-trail

The Seminoles fought three wars from 1817 to 1858 against the United States in a struggle to remain in their Florida ancestral homeland. The State of Florida offers a free 56-page publication that gives the history of the wars and other Florida topics. The publication also includes information and locations of battlefields, cemeteries, museum exhibits, monuments, historical markers, and other sites with direct links to the Seminole Wars.

5 | Miccosukee Resort & Gaming

500 SW 177th Ave., Miami, Florida 33194; 877-242-6464
mrg.miccosukee.com

The Miccosukee tribe was part of the Seminole Nation until the mid-20th century, when they organized as an independent tribe. This resort on the western edge of the metro Miami area is a complete destination featuring modern hotel accommodations, restaurants, gaming, and entertainment venues. While you're there, play a round at one of the Miccosukee Golf & Country Club's three courses, visit an Indian Village, or take an airboat ride. The main Miccosukee reservation is several miles west of the resort on Tamiami Trail (US 41).

6 | Seminole Hard Rock Hotel & Casino

1 Seminole Way, Hollywood, Florida 33314; 866-502-7529
seminolehardrockhollywood.com

This resort is in urban South Florida and close to beaches and other amenities. It features a large hotel and gaming opportunities, including more than 2,000 slot machines. Entertainment is constantly on offer at the 3,500-seat Hard Rock Event Center. There are several restaurants on the property, including the Hard Rock Cafe. Outdoor activities include a beach club with a pool and bar.

Dolphins cavorting in the ocean (photographed by Gerald Marella/Shutterstock)

FLORIDA'S MILD CLIMATE makes it home to an amazing variety of animals. Millions of birds stop by on their annual migratory journeys and a similar number stay here year-round. The state is surrounded by salt water and is home to multitudes of dolphins, a friendly and smart mammal. Manatees, also known as sea cows, are comfortable in the warmer waters around the state. They can't survive in waters below 60 degrees F., so they congregate in various warmer waters around the state in the cold months. There are countless opportunities in Florida to observe and interact with these creatures, especially around Florida's many springs.

BIRDS, DOLPHINS, MANATEES, AND MORE

1 Butterfly World

Tradewinds Park, 3600 W. Sample Road, Coconut Creek, Florida 33073; 954-977-4400
butterflyworld.com

Opened in 1988, Butterfly World is located about 45 minutes north of Fort Lauderdale in Tradewinds Park. Home to more than 20,000 live butterflies, it is the largest butterfly park in the world. It also has the country's largest free-flight hummingbird aviary.

2 Crystal River Manatee Swim

American Pro Diving Center, 821 US 19, Crystal River, Florida 34429; 352-563-0041
americanprodiving.com

Crystal River is a small town 70 miles north of Tampa where West Indian manatees like to congregate in crystal-clear waters where the temperature is 72°F. Manatees cannot survive in water that is colder than 60°F, so this location is perfect for them. American Pro Diving Center offers several snorkel tours where you can visit with these giant, gentle creatures. The best time to visit is November–March, when you can swim with the manatees or just observe them from a boat or a dock in Kings Bay.

3 J. N. Ding Darling National Wildlife Refuge

1 Wildlife Drive, Sanibel, Florida 33957; 239-472-1100
fws.gov/refuge/jn_ding_darling

Located on Sanibel Island, this 6,400-acre refuge is part of the National Wildlife Refuge System. It is named for cartoonist Jay Norwood "Ding" Darling. The refuge was established in 1945 to protect one of the country's largest undeveloped mangrove ecosystems and is well known for its migratory bird populations. You can learn more at the Visitor & Education Center, view birds and wildlife on the Indigo Trail, and explore the Bailey Tract wetland.

4 The Florida Aquarium

701 Channelside Drive, Tampa, Florida 33602; 813-273-4000
flaquarium.org

The kid-friendly Florida Aquarium often appears on lists of the country's best aquariums. The museum has many innovative ways to tell visitors all about the ecological cycles of Florida's unique water systems. Interactive programs such as "Heart of the Sea Swim" and "Dive with the Sharks" let you safely swim with sharks and other fish and even schmooze with penguins. The aquarium also has an outdoor fun zone with a splash pad, sandboxes, and other activities for the kids.

5 Gulfarium Marine Adventure Park

1010 Miracle Strip Pkwy. SE, Fort Walton Beach, Florida 32548; 850-243-9046
gulfarium.com

Since 1955, Gulfarium has sought to inspire its guests to respect and preserve marine life by providing educational and entertaining experiences for people of all ages. The numerous animal encounters offered include those with dolphins, stingrays, gators, reptiles, turtles, penguins, seals, sea lions, and birds. The even have an experience called Breakfast with the Dolphins. Most of the encounters require a reservation.

6 Farm Tours of Ocala

801 SW 60th Ave., Ocala, Florida 32668; 352-895-9302
farmtoursofocala.com

Here you will enjoy a 3.25-hour guided tour of the working farms in Ocala, one of only four major thoroughbred centers in the world. Considered the Horse Capital of the World, Marion County produced American Pharoah, Triple Crown Winner of 2015; Nyquist, winner of the 2016 Kentucky Derby; and other winning horses. On the tour, you'll go behind the scenes and chat with the professionals who train and care for these thoroughbreds.

7 Jungle Island

1111 Parrot Jungle Trail, Miami, Florida 33132; 305-400-7000
jungleisland.com

Jungle Island has been around for more than 75 years in one form or another. Once called Parrot Jungle and located south of Miami, it was famous for letting birds fly free—without cages. The attraction moved to its current location on downtown's Watson Island in 2003 and changed its name to Jungle Island in 2007. It is home to more than 300 birds and other exotic animals, including rare twin orangutans. The birds still fly free.

8 Marineland

9600 Ocean Shore Blvd., St. Augustine, Florida 32080; 904-471-1111
marineland.net

Marineland was founded in 1938 as Marine Studios and was the filming location of many movies. The name was later changed to Marineland, and the first dolphin performances were held here. Today there are no shows where dolphins perform before large audiences, but visitors can interact with dolphins by swimming with them or assisting a trainer in working and playing with the animals. There are also tours and exhibits where you can get a close look at other sea life, including eels, rays, octopi, sea turtles, and sharks.

9 Miami Seaquarium

4400 Rickenbacker Causeway, Miami, Florida 33149; 305-361-5705
miamiseaquarium.com

Miami Seaquarium—filming location for the TV show *Flipper*—is a 38-acre attraction that offers many child-friendly experiences that the entire family will enjoy. You can see and interact with dolphins, sea lions, sting rays, sharks, birds, fish, and even penguins. Watch the animals perform and learn about their lifestyle at shows such as the Flipper Dolphin Show and the Manatee Exhibit. And for a hands-on, behind-the-scenes experience, you can participate in the Trainer for a Day program. The Seaquarium is open 365 days a year.

10 Retirement Home for Horses at Mill Creek Farm

20307 NW CR 235A, Alachua, Florida 32615; 386-462-1001
millcreekfarm.org

The owners of Mill Creek Farm wanted to do something to help horses too old to be ridden or used in various businesses and police departments. They also wanted to help bring rescued horses that had been abused and saved by the SPCA or other humane societies. The farm, open to visitors on Saturdays, has more than 335 rolling acres of tree-lined pastureland for the horses to wander around freely. There are about 100 horses living there at any given time. You can meet some of them for an admission fee of two carrots.

11 Mote Marine Laboratory & Aquarium

1600 Ken Thompson Pkwy., Sarasota, Florida 34236; 941-388-4441
mote.org

Mote is an independent research institution that originally specialized in the study of sharks but in recent years has greatly increased its scope. Its scientists now study the population dynamics of manatees, dolphins, sea turtles, sharks, and coral reefs.

Visitors are welcome to enjoy the working aquarium, which has two touch tanks, a 135,000-gallon shark habitat, and more than 100 species of marine life.

12 Sarasota Jungle Gardens

3701 Bayshore Road, Sarasota, Florida 34234; 941-355-5305
sarasotajunglegardens.com

Sarasota Jungle Gardens is a 10-acre tropical site that is home to more than 200 native and exotic animals, including birds of prey, parrots, macaws, primates, small mammals, dozens of snakes, lizards, iguanas, alligators, crocodiles, and other reptiles. A favorite of visitors is the population of Florida pink flamingos. The flamingos are friendly and often greet guests personally and face-to-face. One may feed them by hand or just enjoy watching them strut by.

13 Seacrest Wolf Preserve

3449 Bonnett Pond Road, Chipley, Florida 32428; 850-773-2897
seacrestwolfpreserve.org

At this preserve, you can become part of the pack as you walk through large natural habitats that are home to gray, Arctic, and British Columbian wolves. The hands-on experience allows visitors as young as age 10 to interact with and learn about this amazing species. Saturday Wolf Encounter Tours last approximately 3.5–4 hours, with a break along the way, as well as places to stop and rest. All tours are by reservation only; call the preserve to schedule one.

A sculpture at The Ringling Museum of Art (photographed by BrittanySed/Shutterstock)

THE ARTS IN FLORIDA include a wide variety of forms that reflect the state's diverse culture. In addition to hundreds of private art galleries, Florida has a large variety of museums ranging from fine art to sidewalk art. From street musicians and symphony orchestras to Broadway musicals in modern performing arts centers, you will find it here. Folk music is part of the cultural fabric, and the state is home to the annual Florida Folk Festival. Dozens of community theaters add to the entertainment opportunities across the state.

THE ARTS

1 Appleton Museum of Art

College of Central Florida, 4333 E. Silver Springs Blvd., Ocala, Florida 34470; 352-291-4455
appletonmuseum.org

The Appleton is a stunning example of classically inspired architecture built of Italian travertine marble. Of the museum's 81,610 square feet museum, 30,000 are devoted to gallery space for the permanent collections, which include examples from America, Asia, Africa, and Iran. The museum also houses a 250-seat auditorium, an art library, three art studio/classroom spaces, and a courtyard café.

2 Artis—Naples

5833 Pelican Bay Blvd., Naples, Florida 34108; 239-597-1900
artisnaples.org

The 8.5-acre Artis—Naples complex includes The Baker Museum (currently closed while undergoing repairs and an expansion to be completed in November 2019) and the performing home of the Naples Philharmonic. The orchestra performs a full schedule each season, and other entertainment is featured as well, including Broadway musicals and dance. The museum's permanent collection includes American, European, and Mexican artists. Special exhibitions include some of the most famous artists in the world.

3 Asolo Repertory Theatre

5555 N. Tamiami Trail, Sarasota, Florida 34243; 941-351-8000
asolorep.org

Asolo Repertory Theatre is one of the most recognized cultural organizations in Florida. It stages up to 15 productions every season, ranging from new plays to reinterpretations of classical and contemporary works. This theater is an important part of Sarasota's arts scene and has a large resident staff of more than 100, including artists and technical craftspeople. Its resident acting company is complemented by award-winning directors, designers, and guest artists who come from all over the world.

4 Broward Center for the Performing Arts

201 SW Fifth Ave., Fort Lauderdale, Florida 33312; 954-462-0222
browardcenter.org

The Broward is in a parklike setting overlooking the New River in downtown Fort Lauderdale. It is ranked in the top 10 most-visited theaters in the world. More than 700,000 patrons enjoy the center's more than 700 performances each year. Among these are Broadway musicals, ballet, operas, concerts, plays, lectures, and workshops. Additional educational events serve more than 150,000 students each year.

5 Cummer Museum

829 Riverside Ave., Jacksonville, Florida 32204; 904-356-6857
cummermuseum.org

The Cummer has one of the finest permanent art collections in Florida, with nearly 5,000 objects dating from 2100 B.C. through modern times and several special collections, such as the Wark Collection of Early Meissen Porcelain. The museum's 2.5-acre garden is a historic example of early 20th-century design. Reflecting pools, fountains, arbors, and sculptures complement the majestic Cummer Oak, whose canopy spans more than 150 feet. This oak is one of the oldest trees in Jacksonville.

6 The Dali Museum

1 Dali Blvd., St. Petersburg, Florida 33701; 727-823-3767
thedali.org

The Dali is first and foremost an "artist's museum" built to showcase the art, archives, and life history of a single artist, in this case, Salvador Dali. Although Dali is most famous for his works of surrealist art, visitors come away from this museum with a new appreciation of how talented in all genres of art he truly was. The permanent collection includes sculpture, prints, photographs, works on paper, paintings, and more. The breadth of his talent was truly amazing.

7 Dr. Phillips Center for the Performing Arts

445 S. Magnolia Ave., Orlando, Florida 32801; 844-513-2014
drphillipscenter.org

Dr. Phillips Center is a hub in downtown Orlando for international, national, and local artists, as well as a community outreach center. The two-block center includes the Walt Disney Theater, the Alexis & Jim Pugh Theater, the DeVos Family Room, the Seneff Arts Plaza, and many other spaces set aside for private events. A school of the arts is also in the complex. From Broadway musicals to ballet, comedy acts, and children's shows, this center has become a tourist destination that locals also love.

8 Florida Theatre

128 E. Forsyth St., Jacksonville, Florida 32202; 904-355-5661
floridatheatre.com

The Florida Theatre is a historic movie theater in downtown Jacksonville. First opened in 1927, it is on the National Register of Historic Places. After numerous renovations, it is now a local and regional center for the performing arts. In addition to offering 200 cultural and entertainment events each year, including ballet, opera, pop, jazz, rock, country, blues, plays, and movies, the theater also serves as a venue for school graduations and charity events that support local churches, hospitals, and civic groups.

9 Kravis Center for the Performing Arts

701 Okeechobee Blvd., West Palm Beach, Florida 33401; 561-833-8300
kravis.org

Located in downtown West Palm Beach, the Kravis Center offers an extensive schedule of events that includes Broadway musicals, famous entertainers, and numerous educational events for the community. A concert hall, two black box theaters, and an events facility comprise the center. In 2016 the Kravis became the first performing arts center in the world to install and feature a custom-designed digital organ in its productions.

10 Lake Placid Murals

Lake Placid Chamber/Mural Gallery, 18 N. Oak St., Lake Placid, Florida 33852; 863-465-4335
tourlakeplacid.com

Downtown Lake Placid has one of the largest outdoor art displays in Florida. These displays are in the form of murals on building walls that celebrate the history of the area. At last count, there were 47 historic murals. In addition to the murals, the local mural society has added nearly 100 pieces of artwork throughout the town. In 2013, Lake Placid won the award of America's Most Interesting Town after a nationwide search by *Reader's Digest*.

11 The Mennello Museum of American Art

900 E. Princeton St., Orlando, Florida 32803; 407-246-4278
mennellomuseum.org

The Mennello, located in Loch Haven Cultural Park, offers visitors green space, lake views, and walking trails. The museum's mission is to preserve, display, and interpret the permanent collection of paintings by Earl Cunningham, a 20th-century American folk artist who painted mostly landscapes of the Atlantic Coast. It also features ever-changing exhibits from other outstanding traditional and contemporary American artists across a broad range of disciplines.

12 The Ringling Museum of Art

5401 Bayshore Road, Sarasota, Florida 34243; 941-359-5700
ringling.org/museum-art

The John and Mable Ringling Museum of Art is the official art museum for the State of Florida. The huge museum contains 21 galleries of European paintings as well as many pieces of Asian, American, and contemporary art. All told, there are more than 28,000 objects in the museum. The Ringling complex includes the art museum, a circus museum, the Asolo Repertory Theater, and Ca'd'Zan, the mansion of John and Mable Ringling.

13 Wynwood Walls

Wynwood Art District, Miami, Florida; 305-531-4411
thewynwoodwalls.com

Wynwood is an area close to downtown Miami and is one of the world's largest outdoor street art museums. The walls of the buildings in Wynwood are decorated by constantly changing murals by some of the world's most gifted and famous graffiti and street artists. You can either walk the neighborhood on your own or sign up for a private walking tour led by local artists.

A laboratory at Edison and Ford Winter Estates (photographed by Kristina Yu/Shutterstock)

THERE ARE MUSEUMS IN FLORIDA for just about any interest you might have. From fine Tiffany art to the bizarre collections in a Believe it or Not museum, you name it and it is probably somewhere in the state. Museums range from the serious, such as the state museums of history and natural history, to sports-themed and automobile-oriented museums, and contain some of the most interesting **artifacts** in Florida, such as recovered shipwrecked Spanish treasure.

MUSEUMS

1 Albin Polasek Museum & Sculpture Gardens

633 Osceola Ave., Winter Park, Florida 32789; 407-647-6294
polasek.org

Albin Polasek (1879–1965) was one of America's foremost sculptors. He retired to Winter Park in 1950 and designed his home with a functioning sculpture studio. A few months after retirement, he suffered a stroke and used a wheelchair for the remainder of his life, yet he was still able to complete 18 major works here before he died. In 1961 his home and gallery were first opened to the public. The sculpture gardens are colorful and lush, with many native Florida and subtropical plants.

2 Don Garlits Museum of Drag Racing

13700 SW 16th Ave., Ocala, Florida 34473; 352-245-8661
garlits.com

"Big Daddy" Don Garlits is a legend in the world of drag racing. His series of 34 hand-built race cars propelled him to 144 national event wins. The Garlits museum has 90 race cars on display in the Drag Race building, as well as 50 other cars in the Antique Car collection. The museum is also home to the International Drag Racing Hall of Fame and includes cars and memorabilia from other famous names in the sport of drag racing. Call a few days in advance to arrange a private, behind-the-scenes tour with "Big Daddy" himself.

3 Edison and Ford Winter Estates

2350 McGregor Blvd., Fort Myers, Florida 33901; 239-334-7419
edisonfordwinterestates.org

See inside the side-by-side homes of Thomas Edison and Henry Ford on the Caloosahatchee River in Fort Myers. The combined property also includes Edison's 20 acres of gardens, his botanic research laboratory, and the 15,000-square-foot Edison Ford Museum, which contains inventions, artifacts, and Edison's Model T, a gift from Ford.

There are also many displays outlining the biographies of the two men. The entire site is a Florida Historic Landmark and hosts many events, including weddings, corporate meetings, and educational programs.

4 Florida Museum of Natural History

University of Florida Cultural Plaza, 3215 Hull Road, Gainesville, Florida 32611; 352-846-2000
floridamuseum.ufl.edu

This museum on the campus of the University of Florida is the official natural history museum of the state. The permanent exhibits focus on the flora, fauna, fossils, and historical people of Florida. An example of the size of this museum is the butterfly and moth collection, which contains 10 million specimens. The mammalogy collection has more than 30,000 specimens, as well as more than 2 million fish specimens. Admission is free (though there is a cover charge for featured exhibits and the Butterfly Rainforest), and one could easily spend a week or even a month and not be able to see everything.

5 Jacksonville Museum of Science & History

1025 Museum Circle, Jacksonville, Florida 32207; 904-396-6674
themosh.org

Known locally as MOSH, this is Jacksonville's most-visited museum, specializing in science and local history. The main exhibit changes quarterly, and the museum is also home to the Bryan-Gooding Planetarium. Interactive exhibits help you learn about your own body's systems. There are also interactive energy exhibits and several animal encounters. An unusual feature of this museum is its science and history boat tours on the adjacent St. Johns River.

6 John Gorrie State Museum

46 Sixth St., Apalachicola, Florida 32320; 850-653-9347
floridastateparks.org/parks-and-trails/john-gorrie-museum-state-park

This state park's main exhibits feature the history of the Apalachicola area and focus specifically on the life and invention of John Gorrie. This museum should actually be a shrine worshipped by all Floridians, as Dr. Gorrie was a pioneer in the development of air-conditioning. A physician, a scientist, an inventor, and a humanitarian, he received the first US patent for mechanical refrigeration in 1851. His ice-making machine was the result of his search for a way to cool his patients' rooms.

7 McLarty Treasure Museum

Sebastian Inlet State Park, 9700 S. FL A1A, Melbourne Beach, Florida 32951;
321-984-4852
floridastateparks.org/parks-and-trails/sebastian-inlet-state-park

The small McLarty Treasure Museum, part of Sebastian Inlet State Park, takes you back to the days of the Spanish treasure-fleet voyages from the Caribbean to Spain more than 300 years ago. Eleven ships were lost in a hurricane in 1715, and salvagers are still working to recover gold, silver, and jewels that were lost from the fleet. The museum features artifacts, displays, and an observation deck that overlooks the Atlantic Ocean.

8 Morse Museum

445 N. Park Ave., Winter Park, Florida 32789; 407-645-5311
morsemuseum.org

With more than 19,000 square feet of public exhibition space, the Charles Hosmer Morse Museum of American Art is home to the world's most comprehensive collection of works by Louis Comfort Tiffany (1848–1933), including not only jewelry and leaded-glass lamps and windows but also pottery, paintings, and art glass. The chapel interior he designed for the 1893 World's Columbian Exposition in Chicago was installed in 1999, four years after the museum's opening. The holdings also include art and architectural elements from Tiffany's Long Island country estate, along with works by his contemporaries, with a particular focus on the Arts and Crafts style.

9 Museum of Florida History

500 S. Bronough, Tallahassee, Florida 32399; 850-245-6400
museumoffloridahistory.com

This is the official history museum of the State of Florida, highlighting artifacts and eras unique to Florida and the roles Floridians have played nationally and globally. Exhibits change frequently and have featured Florida artists, quintessential Florida imagery, posters from films made in the state, Seminole history, and more. The museum also operates The Knott House Museum, where the Emancipation Proclamation was read in 1865, declaring freedom for all slaves in greater Tallahassee.

.0 National Navy UDT-SEAL Museum

3300 N. FL A1A, North Hutchinson Island, Fort Pierce, Florida 34949; 772-595-5845
navysealmuseum.org

The National Navy SEAL Museum has an unusual collection of artifacts and exhibits dedicated to the famous warriors of the US Navy SEAL teams and their predecessors, the Underwater Demolition Teams (UDT). Exhibits include a special operations boat; a Black Hawk helicopter; weaponry; and even a display about Barry, a canine who bears the title of Naval Special Warfare Group Two's "first dog," who served in over 225 combat missions.

.1 Orange County Regional History Center

65 E. Central Blvd., Orlando, Florida 32801; 407-836-8500
thehistorycenter.org

This museum in downtown Orlando focuses on the history of Central Florida. Among the exhibits are those chronicling African-American history, aviation, and cattle and citrus. Also featured are Florida tourism history, history of the Spanish era, and the American Indian tribes who lived in Florida before the arrival of the Europeans in the 1500s. The region's flora, fauna, and geography are explained, as is the area's transformation by theme parks. A furnished 19th-century pioneer cabin is also on display.

.2 Ripley's Believe It or Not!

19 San Marco Ave., St. Augustine, Florida 32084; 904-824-1606
ripleys.com/staugustine

This is a museum you must see to believe. Housed in an 1887 castle-like building, it specializes in bizarre events and objects that are so strange they defy belief, including real shrunken heads, a three-story Erector Set Ferris wheel, and a wax replica of the world's tallest man. Opened in 1950 as the first permanent Believe It or Not! museum, it is now one of 30 Ripley's "odditoriums," but I like this one the most.

13 The Lightner Museum

75 King St., St. Augustine, Florida 32084; 904-824-2874
lightnermuseum.org

Lightner Museum is in the former Alcazar Hotel, which was built in 1888. It has a large collection of fine and decorative 19th century art, much of it from the Gilded Age. The first floor houses a Victorian village with shop fronts representing period stores selling period goods. There are examples of cut glass, stained glass, and period furniture pieces. There is even a small mummy, a model steam engine, a player piano, and a golden elephant carrying the earth on its back.

14 The Revs Institute

2500 S. Horseshoe Drive, Naples, Florida 34104; 239-687-7387
revsinstitute.org

This museum was only recently opened to the public. It houses the formerly private Miles Collier Collection, one of the world's premier auto collections, containing more than 100 beautiful automobiles manufactured between 1896 and 1995. Each car in the collection is rare and historically significant, the flagship vehicle being the 1939 Mercedes W154 Grand Prix (the Silver Arrow).

The Lightner Museum (photographed by Paul Brennan/Shutterstock)

A Florida beach (photographed by Fotoluninate LLC/Shutterstock)

FLORIDA HAS ONE OF THE LONGEST saltwater shorelines in the United States, and the Environmental Protection Agency says the state has 570 beaches, with a total beach length of 902 miles. We don't know who can challenge that number, but it doesn't really matter. No matter what kind of beach you are looking for, Florida probably has it. From sunbathing to long walks, treasure hunting, or searching for unique seashells, you can find it here.

BEACHES AND SEASHELLS

4 Various locations

1 Anna Maria Island

Anna Maria Island Chamber of Commerce, 5313 Gulf Drive, Holmes Beach, Florida 34217; 941-778-1541
annamariaislandchamber.org

The beaches on the Gulf of Mexico have powdery white sand and are soft on your feet, and Anna Maria Island's are no exception. The sand is composed of very fine quartz crystals, and this keeps it from getting too hot to lie or walk on, making it great for walking and sunbathing. The surf is rarely too rough; it's just wavy enough for a boogie board or to enjoy splashing around in the shallow water. Another plus is that, unlike many other beaches in Florida, Anna Maria Island's are not lined with high-rise condos.

2 Bailey-Matthews National Shell Museum

3075 Sanibel Captiva Road, Sanibel, Florida 33957; 239-395-2233
shellmuseum.org

My grandmother loved to collect shells. She died too soon to experience this museum, which opened to the public in 1995. The museum operates as a reference center for scientists and amateur collectors. Shells from all over the world are on display; many of them are from Sanibel and Captiva. The museum also has a memorial garden dedicated to actor Raymond Burr, who owned an island in Fiji and helped raise funds to build the museum. Scientists lead daily hour-long beach walks to teach you about local shells.

3 Caladesi Island

Offshore Island, Dunedin, Florida 34698; 727-469-5918
floridastateparks.org/parks-and-trails/caladesi-island-state-park

Caladesi is one of the few remaining untouched islands on the Florida Gulf Coast. It is accessible by private boat, the Caladesi Island Ferry, or by walking from Clearwater Beach. The ferry dock is on Honeymoon Island, connected by causeway to the town of Dunedin. The island's 3 miles of unspoiled, pristine white sand beaches make it perfect for swimming, sunbathing, shelling, boating, fishing, and snorkeling. You can also enjoy kayaking through a 3-mile mangrove trail or camping on your boat at the marina.

4 Sand Castle Lessons

Beach Sand Sculptures, various locations from Fort Morgan, Alabama, to Panama City; 303-681-2631
beachsandsculptures.com

Most people have tried to build a sand castle at least once in their lives. These lessons take this skill to a whole new level. The beautiful beaches around Destin have attracted businesses that will teach you how to build your ultimate sand castle. You can either have an expert build one for you or learn how to build one yourself. Lessons are offered all along the northwest Florida coast, from Fort Morgan, Alabama, east to Panama City. The website will give you further details.

5 Fort De Soto Park

3500 Pinellas Bayway S, Tierra Verde, Florida 33715; 727-582-2100
pinellascounty.org/park/05_ft_desoto.htm

Fort De Soto Park is the largest park in the Pinellas County park system, with 1,136 acres. Visitors reach it from the mainland via FL 679. The five interconnected islands that make up the park are among the most natural environment in Florida and feature 3 miles of some of the most beautiful white sand beaches in the United States. Things to do include visiting the historic fort, camping, swimming, hiking, kayaking, biking, and fishing from a park pier.

6 Little Talbot Island State Park

12157 Heckscher Drive, Jacksonville, Florida 32226; 904-251-2320
floridastateparks.org/parks-and-trails/little-talbot-island-state-park

This park is about 25 miles northeast of Jacksonville on one of the few remaining barrier islands on Florida's east coast. You will enjoy nature at its finest, with maritime forests, desertlike dunes, and pristine salt marshes. The streams on the west side of the park as well as the Atlantic surf provide great opportunities for beachcombing and fishing. Catches include trout, redfish, flounder, and black drum. There is also a campground in the park.

7 Tigertail Beach Park

430 Hernando Drive, Marco Island, Florida 34145; 239-252-4000
tinyurl.com/tigertailbeach

Marco Island is highly developed, but Tigertail Beach is a tranquil, wild beach in the middle of it all. The developed part of the beach park has a parking lot, changing rooms, and a snack bar. The park faces a shallow saltwater lagoon. You can either use this beach or wade across the lagoon to another one. Sometimes the water is waist-deep or more, but once you have crossed you will find a 3-mile-long beach made of soft white sand. Most of the beach is wild, and all of it is totally undeveloped.

8 Sanibel and Captiva Islands

1159 Causeway Road, Sanibel Island, Florida 33957; 239-472-1080
sanibel-captiva.org

My grandmother lived in Venice but loved to travel to Sanibel Island for the magnificent shells she would find on the beach. She spent many joyous hours in the "Sanibel stoop," the bent-over posture assumed by shell seekers. There are other things to do on Sanibel, of course, including biking, fishing, bird-watching, boating, golfing, and snorkeling. But shelling remains a popular activity for thousands of visitors. In 2017, *Travel & Leisure* magazine ranked Sanibel Island the best shelling beach in North America.

9 Topsail Hill Preserve State Park

7525 W. FL 30A, Santa Rosa Beach, Florida 32459; 850-267-8330
floridastateparks.org/park/topsail-hill

When you are offshore on a boat in the Gulf of Mexico, the tall white sand dunes in this park resemble the sails of sailing ships. The tallest of the majestic dunes, which stretch for 3 miles and are made of pristine white quartz sand, rises 25 feet above sea level. The beaches are among the best in Florida for swimming, fishing, sunbathing, or just beachcombing, and the adjacent park is a bird-watching and hiking paradise.

Seashells on Sanibel Island (photographed by EQRoy/Shutterstock)

Beaches
and Seashells

Rainbow Springs (photographed by Robert Greeley/Shutterstock)

FLORIDA HAS ABOUT 1,000 known freshwater springs, 33 of which are first-magnitude springs discharging more than 100 cubic feet of water per second. The largest springs discharge groundwater from the Floridan aquifer, a limestone formation underlying much of the state. Most spring water is at a constant temperature of 68–72°F. Many Florida springs support unique ecosystems, and they also flow into streams and rivers that depend on the flow of fresh water. Springs are wonderful swimming holes but also a great place to see manatees, alligators, otters, and a large variety of fish, birds, and turtles.

SPRINGS

1 Alexander Springs

Alexander Springs Recreational Area, 49525 County Road 445, Altoona, Florida; 352-669-3522
recreation.gov/camping/campgrounds/234032

Alexander Springs and the recreation area named for it are in the Ocala National Forest, the southernmost and oldest national forest east of the Mississippi River. The recreation area offers camping, swimming, canoeing, scuba diving, hiking, birding, and wildlife viewing. Alexander Springs is among 27 first-magnitude springs in Florida. (A first-magnitude spring discharges at least 100 cubic feet of water per second.) The clear water is a constant 72°F and has a sandy bottom.

2 Blue Spring State Park

2100 W. French Ave., Orange City, Florida 32763; 386-775-3663
floridastateparks.org/parks-and-trails/blue-spring-state-park

This park is a favorite place to watch the West Indian manatee. Hundreds of these gentle animals make the springs their winter home. The springs' constant 72°F temperature also attracts scores of humans enjoying swimming, snorkeling, fishing, and paddling in the clear, unspoiled waters. There are plenty of overlooks and observation points in the park, but it is best to visit the park early in the day to beat the crowds.

3 Crystal River National Wildlife Refuge

1502 SE Kings Bay Drive, Crystal River, Florida 34429; 352-563-2088
www.fws.gov/refuge/crystal_river

Crystal River is one of several wildlife refuges in the area managed by the U.S. Fish & Wildlife Service. Located in the last unspoiled and undeveloped spring habitat in Kings Bay, which forms the headwaters of the Crystal River, it is the only refuge created specifically for the protection of the threatened Florida manatee. Nearly 600 manatees spend the winter in Kings Bay. During this season, the most popular manatee-viewing opportunity the refuge offers is from a boardwalk. There are also dozens of commercial ventures in the area that offer guided tours, kayak rentals, and educational opportunities.

4 De Leon Springs State Park

601 Ponce de Leon Blvd., De Leon Springs, Florida 32130; 386-985-4212
floridastateparks.org/parks-and-trails/de-leon-springs-state-park

De Leon Springs State Park is known for its swimming area and restaurant, but the visitor center and other displays are also a rich source of cultural information, looking back 6,000 years into the park's history. Take an eco-history boat tour on which you may see gators, bald eagles, otters, or wading birds. An unusual and popular feature at the park is the pancake breakfast or lunch at the Sugar Mill Restaurant, where you prepare your own pancakes at the table. You can also walk a 4-mile trail through the hardwood forests and cypress swamps and sometimes see wild deer, turkeys, and maybe even a black bear.

5 Ichetucknee Springs State Park

12087 SW US 27, Fort White, Florida 32038; 386-497-4690
floridastateparks.org/parks-and-trails/ichetucknee-springs-state-park

Tubing on the Ichetucknee River is a generations-old Florida tradition. The crystal-clear, spring-fed river flows 6 miles through shaded hammocks and wetlands before it joins the Santa Fe River. Most native Floridians know that this river is the real Florida, the way it used to be. It is always cool under the lush tree canopy that shades this stream. From the end of May until early September, tubing down the river is the premier activity in the area. You can also picnic, snorkel, canoe, hike, or just chill out.

6 Rainbow Springs State Park

19158 Southwest 81st Place Road, Dunnellon, Florida 34432; 352-465-8555
floridastateparks.org/parks-and-trails/rainbow-springs-state-park

Rainbow Springs is Florida's fourth-largest spring and forms the headwaters of the Rainbow River. From the 1930s through the 1970s, it was the site of a popular, privately owned attraction and, after closing for several years, reopened as a state park in the 1990s. At the park's main entrance, at the headsprings, you can swim in the freshwater river, rent canoes and kayaks, view waterfalls and gardens, and enjoy a picnic area with grills and pavilions. There are also campsites. Tubes are available farther down the river for floating downstream.

7 Silver Springs State Park

1425 NE 58th Ave., Ocala, Florida 34470; 352-236-7148
floridastateparks.org/silversprings

For many years Silver Springs was Florida's most popular commercial tourist attraction. It was famous for its glass-bottom boats and the clarity of the spring-fed Silver River. Many movies were filmed here as well. Lloyd Bridges filmed parts of 100 episodes of television series *Sea Hunt* here. Over the years, the springs and attraction became a state park. You can still enjoy riding on the glass-bottom boats, paddling in a kayak, or just staring in amazement at the crystal-clear blue depths of Silver Springs. You can camp here, visit the museum, or eat in the restaurant. Birds and flowers abound, and every now and then a monkey appears, descended from some that escaped from a tour-boat operator, who brought them to the area to create a Tarzan-themed attraction that never came to fruition.

8 Wakulla Springs State Park

465 Wakulla Park Drive, Wakulla Springs, Florida 32327; 850-561-7276
floridastateparks.org/parks-and-trails/edward-ball-wakulla-springs-state-park

The official name of this park is Edward Ball Wakulla Springs State Park, and it is named after the Florida financier who built a lodge on the property and developed the land as an attraction aimed at preserving wildlife. Many movies were made in these springs, including a *Tarzan* film starring Johnny Weissmuller. The constant 70°F waters are a wonderful treat on hot summer days. You can also take a 45-minute riverboat tour on which you will usually see alligators, an occasional manatee, and many bird species. You can book a stay at Ball's historic Lodge at Wakulla Springs. The magnificence of the lodge alone is worth a trip to this park.

9 | Warm Mineral Springs

12200 San Servando Ave., North Port, Florida 34287; 941-426-1692
cityofnorthport.com/visitors/visit-north-port/warm-mineral-springs-park

Warm Mineral Springs is unique for its year-round temperature of 85°F, much warmer than most Florida springs. It is estimated that the waters contain 51 minerals, one of the highest mineral contents of any natural spring in the United States. The springs have been a city park since 2014, but for many years before that, a steady stream of visitors came from around the world for the alleged therapeutic effects of the water. Local legend has it that Ponce de Leon visited and that it was the basis for his legendary Fountain of Youth. You can either swim in the water or just sit and soak it up. A variety of spa services, including massages and facials, are also available; call ahead to make a reservation.

10 | Wekiwa Springs State Park

1800 Wekiwa Circle, Apopka, Florida 32712; 407-553-4383
floridastateparks.org/parks-and-trails/wekiwa-springs-state-park

Wekiwa Springs has been a popular recreational spot for Orlando area residents and tourists for more than 100 years. It is so popular that on many days from May through October they have to close it when the maximum capacity of 250 cars has been reached. The clear, cool springs feed the Wekiwa River, and in addition to a large swimming area, there are miles of trails for hiking, biking, or horseback riding. Canoes and kayaks can be rented in the park, and you can paddle along the Wekiwa River and Rock Springs Run. A full-facility campground is also located in a quiet section of the park.

St. Augustine Lighthouse (photographed by Mary Terriberry/Shutterstock)

FLORIDA LIGHTHOUSES are among the state's oldest structures and make an entertaining destination for a Florida day trip. All of them have interesting stories to tell, and some can be visited by tourists. The oldest lighthouse on mainland Florida is the one in St. Augustine that was built in 1824. The tallest in Florida is at Ponce de Leon Inlet south of Daytona Beach. It is 175 feet tall and one of the tallest in the United States. Some of Florida's lighthouses allow visitors to climb to the top, and a few also serve as popular wedding locations.

LIGHTHOUSES

1 Amelia Island Lighthouse

215 O'Hagan Lane, Fernandina Beach, Florida 32034 (tours leave from Atlantic Recreation Center, 2500 Atlantic Ave.); 904-310-3350
fbfl.us/474/amelia-island-lighthouse-tour

The Amelia Island Lighthouse overlooks Egans Creek and the St. Marys River at its entrance to the Atlantic Ocean. Built in 1838 using materials from a lighthouse formerly located on Georgia's Cumberland Island, it is the oldest existing lighthouse in Florida. The US Coast Guard transferred ownership of it to the City of Fernandina Beach in 2001 and now maintains it as a historical monument. Access is limited by the city as the structure is in a residential neighborhood. It is open to the public on Saturdays from 11 a.m. to 2 p.m., and tours are given on the first and third Wednesday of every month at 10 a.m.

2 Cape Florida Light

Bill Baggs Cape Florida State Park, 1200 S. Crandon Blvd., Key Biscayne, Florida 33149; 305-361-5811
floridastateparks.org/parks-and-trails/bill-baggs-cape-florida-state-park

The Cape Florida Light is on the southern tip of Key Biscayne, southeast of Miami. Built in 1825, it is one of Florida's oldest lighthouses. It operated until 1878, when its role was replaced by a new light offshore at Fowey Rocks. In 1966 the state purchased the property that would later become Bill Baggs Cape Florida State Park, and the Coast Guard reactivated the light in 1978. It was deactivated again in 1992 because of hurricane damage and has been in operation again since 1996. The lighthouse and keeper's quarters have been restored, and the lighthouse is open to the public. Guided tours take place at 10 a.m. and 1 p.m., Thursday–Monday. Climb the 95 steps of the tower for a fantastic view of Key Biscayne and Miami.

3 Crooked River Lighthouse

1975 US 98 W, Carrabelle, Florida 32322; 850-697-2732
crookedriverlighthouse.org

The Crooked River Lighthouse was built in 1895 to guide fishermen, oystermen, and lumber ships through the pass between Dog and St. George Islands. In 1995 the Coast Guard decommissioned the lighthouse and it was headed for auction. A local citizens group formed the Carrabelle Lighthouse Association (CLA) to restore and preserve the lighthouse and open it to the public. The lighthouse is now owned by the City of Carrabelle, and the Keeper's House Museum is open Wednesday–Sunday. A $5 donation or CLA membership allows you to climb to the top of the lighthouse.

4 Gasparilla Island Light

220 Gulf Blvd., Boca Grande, Florida
florida-backroads-travel.com/gasparilla-island-light.html

Originally in service as a range light in Delaware, the Gasparilla Island Light was disassembled in 1921 and put back together in 1927 on Gasparilla Island. It began service in 1932 as the rear entrance range light for Port Boca Grande and was coordinated with the front entrance light about 1 mile offshore (the front light was removed years ago). The Gasparilla Island Light is one of two lighthouses that can be seen today on Gasparilla Island, the other being the Port Boca Grande Lighthouse (see pg. 51), located in Gasparilla Island State Park to the south.

5 Hillsboro Inlet Lighthouse

907 Hillsboro Mile, Hillsboro Beach, Florida 33062; 954-942-2102 (museum)
www.hillsborolighthouse.org

The Hillsboro Lighthouse was built in 1906 and is located on the east side of Hillsboro Inlet. A museum operated by the Hillsboro Lighthouse Preservation Society is located on the west side of the inlet at 2700 N. Ocean Blvd. A statue of the Barefoot Mailman on the lighthouse site memorializes the mail carriers who walked a 80-mile route along the beach in the late 19th century. One of the mailmen disappeared while walking the route in 1887 and was presumed to have either drowned or been killed by an alligator or shark while trying to swim across Hillsboro Inlet. The lighthouse is open periodically for tours, and you are required to take a boat from a nearby dock to visit it. You are permitted to climb the 175-step lighthouse tower on these tours. Call the museum for information on tour dates and times. The museum is open Sunday, Tuesday, Thursday, Friday, and Saturday from 11 a.m. to 3 p.m.

6 Jupiter Inlet Lighthouse

500 Captain Armour's Way, Jupiter, Florida 33469; 561-747-8380
jupiterlighthouse.org

The Jupiter Inlet Lighthouse & Museum has been open to the public since 1973. The tower was first lit in 1860 and has a wonderful view of Jupiter Inlet and the Atlantic Ocean. Tours of the lighthouse grounds and museum, including tower climbs, are available to the public. The lighthouse property also serves as a park and community center for the area and has a busy event schedule. The museum features many exhibits of American Indian and early pioneer culture. Access to the lighthouse is by paid guided tour only and tickets are purchased in the museum.

7 Mount Dora Lighthouse

Grantham Point at Gilbert Park, 311 S. Tremain St., Mount Dora, Florida 32757
fl-mountdora.civicplus.com/facilities/facility/details/gilbert-park-7

The Mount Dora Lighthouse is considered by many purists not to be the real thing—a faux lighthouse, so to speak. The lighthouse is only 35 feet tall and is not open to the public. It is, however, an official registered aid to inland navigation and has become one of Mount Dora's best-known landmarks and photo opportunities. The lighthouse was dedicated in 1988 and is built of stucco-covered brick. Its light guides boaters on Lake Dora safely to the adjacent boat ramps and Mount Dora Boating Center & Marina.

8 Pensacola Lighthouse

2081 Radford Blvd., Pensacola, Florida 32508; 850-393-1561
pensacolalighthouse.org

The Pensacola Lighthouse and Maritime Museum is located on Naval Air Station Pensacola adjacent to the National Naval Aviation Museum. The tower was built in 1859 and has a spectacular view of the Gulf Coast. You can climb up the 177 steps to the top, where the view includes Pensacola Pass, Pensacola Bay, three historic forts, the downtown skyline of Pensacola, and the historic Navy Yard. You can also make a reservation to have front-row seats for a Blue Angels practice. The lighthouse and museum are open to the public daily. All civilian visitors must enter through the Public Gate, located just south of the intersection of Blue Angel Parkway and Gulf Beach Highway, and must present proper photo identification (see website for details).

9 Ponce de Leon Inlet Lighthouse

4931 S. Peninsula Drive, Ponce Inlet, Florida 32127; 386-761-1821
ponceinlet.org

Designated a National Historic Landmark, Ponce de Leon Inlet Lighthouse is on the inlet that connects the Halifax River to the Atlantic Ocean, about 12 miles south of Daytona Beach. It is not only Florida's tallest lighthouse, but also the second-tallest masonry lighthouse in the country, behind the Hatteras Lighthouse on the Outer Banks of North Carolina. The top is 175 feet high and takes 203 steps to climb. Self-guided tour maps are provided, or you can take a guided tour. The view from the top is worth the climb: you will see the high-rise condos and beaches to the north in Daytona Beach and to the south in New Smyrna Beach. The museum has interesting displays of various lights that have been in operation at the lighthouse and displays of the living quarters of the keepers who served there. The lighthouse and museum are open to the public daily except for Thanksgiving and Christmas.

10 Port Boca Grande Lighthouse

880 Belcher Road, Boca Grande, Florida 33921; 941-964-0375
floridastateparks.org/parks-and-trails/gasparilla-island-state-park
barrierislandparkssociety.org/port-boca-grande-lighthouse-museum

Port Boca Grande Lighthouse and museum are located on the south end of Gasparilla Island at Gasparilla Island State Park. The lighthouse was built in 1890 and has been restored nearly to its original condition. It is the oldest structure on Gasparilla Island. The lighthouse museum covers the cultural history of the area from 12,000 B.C. to the present time. One of the museum rooms is a "please touch" area where you can examine local bones, fossils, and shells. The museum also has a gift shop. One of the nicest things about visiting this lighthouse are the gliders on the porch where you can sit and enjoy the beach and the sounds of the sea. The state park is open daily from 8 a.m. to sunset. The hours of operation of the lighthouse and museum vary seasonally.

11 St. Augustine Lighthouse

100 Red Cox Road, St. Augustine, Florida 32080; 904-829-0745
staugustinelighthouse.com

St. Augustine Lighthouse is on Anastasia Island between downtown St. Augustine and the Atlantic Ocean. Built in 1874 on the site of an old Spanish watchtower dating back to the 1500s, the lighthouse is 165 feet above sea level. From the top viewing platform—219 steps up—you see a breathtaking view of St. Augustine, the ocean, the beach, and Salt Run with its boat anchorage. The light is still lit these days and is a pleasant addition to the St. Augustine skyline. The facilities are operated by the St. Augustine Lighthouse and Maritime Museum Inc., which provides a wide variety of educational programs for schoolchildren and coordinates the visits of the many tourists who come each year.

12 St. Marks Lighthouse

1255 Lighthouse Road, St. Marks, FL 32327; 850-925-6121
stmarksrefuge.org/lighthouse.htm

This lighthouse is on the St. Marks National Wildlife Refuge about 25 miles south of Tallahassee. It is the second oldest in Florida and the oldest on Florida's Gulf Coast. The current tower was built in 1842. The nearby town of St. Marks was an important port of entry in the early days of Florida. This lighthouse was built to facilitate entry to the port. The tower and keeper's house were recently restored and are open for tours on the first Friday and Saturday of each month; however, visitors may not climb the tower.

Jupiter Inlet Lighthouse (photographed by Thomas Barrat/Shutterstock)

Vizcaya Museum & Gardens, Miami (photographed by travelview/Shutterstock)

THE OLDEST BUILDINGS IN FLORIDA are in St. Augustine, reflecting the Spanish heritage dating back to 1565. Many architectural masterpieces in the rest of the state were constructed during Florida's Gilded Age of the 1880s and 1890s. Some of the most impressive buildings were built during the real estate boom of the 1920s and are still functioning as hotels or other businesses. Florida also has its share of historic mansions, many of which have been preserved and converted to museums.

HISTORIC BUILDINGS AND ARCHITECTURE

A statue at Ca'D'Zan Mansion (photographed by oceanbluephotography/Shutterstock)

1 The Ancient Spanish Monastery

16711 W. Dixie Hwy., North Miami Beach, Florida 33160; 305-945-1461
spanishmonastery.com

Don't feel tricked, but although it truly is Florida's oldest building, there is a catch. The monastery was actually built in Spain in 1141. It was purchased by William Randolph Hearst, taken apart stone by stone, and shipped to America, finally ending up here in North Miami Beach. The building is more than 400 years older than some of the national historic monuments in St. Augustine. The buildings and grounds are beautiful and have become a popular place for weddings and other special ceremonies. Church services are held on Sundays.

2 The Biltmore

1200 Anastasia Ave., Coral Gables, Florida 33134; 855-311-6903
biltmorehotel.com

The Biltmore is a luxury hotel and resort where you can spend time in magnificent surroundings. Built in 1926 in the Spanish Colonial style, it has been used as a setting for movies and television shows, including *Miami Vice,* and its swimming pool is the largest on the East Coast. The rich and famous have stayed there, including the Duke and Duchess of Windsor, President Franklin D. Roosevelt, Bing Crosby, and even the infamous Al Capone. Activities include golf and cooking classes conducted by the Biltmore Culinary Academy.

3 Bok Tower Gardens

1151 Tower Blvd., Lake Wales, Florida 33853; 863-676-1408
boktowergardens.org

The quiet, serene gardens of Bok Tower are a pleasant contrast to the busy activity of the theme parks in Orlando and elsewhere in Central Florida. This attraction is only an hour and a half from Orlando, but it seems far away from the traffic.

Edward Bok was the editor of *Ladies' Home Journal* and transformed this sandy hill near Lake Wales into one of the most beautiful places in the country. The tropical plantings shade visitors and are home to more than 125 species of birds. The singing tower with its carillon plays concerts every day at 1 p.m. and 3 p.m., and shorter musical pieces at other times during the day. Bok Tower Gardens has also become one of Florida's most popular wedding venues.

4 The Breakers

1 S. County Road, Palm Beach, Florida 33480; 833-777-7610
thebreakers.com

The Breakers is a 538-room hotel and resort on the Atlantic Ocean that was opened in 1896 by Florida railroad tycoon Henry Flagler. If you stay at this resort you will be surrounded by the opulent history of Palm Beach. Many large conferences and conventions are held here, and the hotel has more than 2,000 employees. The architectural design is described as Italian Renaissance inspired by 15th-century Italian villas. The hotel has nine restaurants, two 18-hole golf courses, four swimming pools, and a private beach on the Atlantic Ocean.

5 Ca'd'Zan

5401 Bay Shore Blvd., Sarasota, Florida 34243; 941-359-5700
ringling.org/cadzan

John Ringling made his fortune in the circus business. He and his brothers operated the circus known as "The Greatest Show on Earth." His personal home, Ca'd'Zan (Venetian dialect for "House of John"), is a mansion constructed in the Venetian Gothic style. In addition to the mansion, the Ringling complex includes the Museum of Art (page 25) and the Circus Museum. A museum ticket gets you into both museums, but not into the mansion. You can buy a ticket that includes admission to the museums and a tour of Ca'd'Zan led by a docent. There are many tour and admission options; go to the website before visiting so you can make the right decision about what you want to see and what time you want to see it.

6 Cassadaga Spiritualist Camp

1112 Stevens St., Cassadaga, Florida 32706; 386-228-2880
cassadaga.org

This historic town is on the National Register of Historic Places and has preserved its original roots as a spiritualist camp. There are many Victorian-era cottages and homes in the camp where the spiritualists live and work. There are many mediums in the village, and many self-

proclaimed healers who pride themselves on teaching people to tap into their own ability to heal themselves. There is a hotel on-site that is reportedly home to ghosts, and there is a gift shop with crystals, stones, jewelry, DVDs and CDs, and a large collection of books on spiritualism and metaphysics.

7 Coral Castle

28655 S. Dixie Hwy., Miami, Florida 33033; 305-248-6345
coralcastle.com

Latvian Ed Leedskalnin was about to be married to his 16-year-old sweetheart when she backed out the day before the wedding. Ed was broken-hearted and left for America, ending up in Florida in 1918. He decided to create a monument to his sweetheart and started work on his castle. Ed was just over 5 feet tall and weighed 100 pounds. This fact will amaze you when you see the size of the giant rocks he used to build his monument. All by himself, he carved 1,100 tons of coral rock and moved them into locations on his property. He had no large machinery, and he did most of his work after sunset using lanterns for light. Each section of the wall at Coral Castle is 8 feet tall, 4 feet wide, and 3 feet thick. Ed died without ever revealing the mystery of how he was able to manipulate these giant rocks. He only said he understood the laws of weight and leverage.

8 DeFuniak Springs Historic District

City of DeFuniak Springs, 71 US 90 W, DeFuniak Springs, Florida 32433;
850-892-8500
defuniaksprings.net/1170/historic-district-information

This small Panhandle city has a large collection of Victorian homes and other buildings surrounding a circular lake in the historic downtown area. The town was the summer home from 1884 to 1927 of the Chautauqua Assembly (an educational movement) and the DeFuniak Springs Historic District, along with several individual homes, is listed on the National Register of Historic Places.

9 Flagler Museum (Whitehall)

1 Whitehall Way, Palm Beach, Florida 33480; 561-655-2833
flaglermuseum.us

Whitehall was the luxurious 75-room mansion of railroad tycoon Henry Flagler. When completed in 1902, the *New York Herald* declared it "more wonderful than any palace in Europe, grander and more magnificent than any other private dwelling in the world." Today, Whitehall is a National Historic Landmark. Now open to the public as the Flagler Museum, it features tours, shifting exhibits, and special programs. Many of the original furnishings are still in the building, and there is also a large art collection.

10 Flagler College (Hotel Ponce de Leon)

74 King St., St. Augustine, Florida 32084; 904-823-3378
legacy.flagler.edu/pages/tours

Flagler College is in the former Hotel Ponce de Leon. This building is a memory trip for me, as I spent a New Year's Eve as a guest in this hotel many years ago. The hotel was built by railroad tycoon Henry Flagler in 1888 and is a National Historic Landmark. You can take a tour and explore the courtyard while learning of the hotel's Spanish Renaissance architecture and of the techniques used to construct it. You will also visit the grand lobby with its 68-foot domed ceiling supported by eight ornate oak caryatids. The dining room contains 79 Louis Comfort Tiffany stained glass windows and hand-painted murals on the walls and ceiling. You will also see personal photos and mementos from Henry Flagler and his family.

11 Florida State Capitol

Florida's Capitol Complex, 400 S. Monroe St., Tallahassee, Florida 32399; 850-488-6167
floridacapitol.myflorida.com

Tallahassee became the capital of Florida territory back in 1824 and has held onto this distinction through Statehood and beyond. The old capitol building has been preserved and restored and is next door to the modern tower that serves as the headquarters for Florida's state government. You can take a self-guided tour, the highlight of which is a trip to the 22nd-floor observation deck for a breathtaking view of Tallahassee.

12 Frank Lloyd Wright "Child of the Sun"

Florida Southern College, 111 Lake Hollingsworth Drive, Lakeland, Florida 33801;
863-680-4597
flsouthern.edu/visitors/fllw-visitors.aspx

Florida Southern College in Lakeland is home to 12 buildings designed by Frank Lloyd Wright from 1938 to 1959 and is on the National Register of Historic Places. The structures, together referred to as "Child of the Sun," are still used by students and faculty today. The visitor center has photographs, furniture, and drawings related to Wright's work on the campus, as well as a gift shop. Guided tours of the Wright-designed buildings are offered by appointment. You can also tour the campus on your own; purchase a map at the visitor center.

13 Ocean Drive Art Deco District

The Art Deco Welcome Center, 1001 Ocean Drive, Miami Beach, Florida 33139;
305-672-2014
mdpl.org

The Miami Design Preservation League was established to protect and preserve the Art Deco buildings built in the Streamline Moderne style in Miami Beach during the Great Depression and up to the beginning of World War II. These buildings are complemented by a mix of other designs, some known as Tropical Deco. This part of Miami Beach—known as South Beach—has an interesting mix of well-preserved and functioning hotels, restaurants, and shops with Art Deco, Mediterranean Revival, and Miami Modern styles. Walking tours can be arranged, or you can explore the neighborhood on your own.

14 Oldest House Museum Complex

14 St. Francis St., St. Augustine, Florida 32084; 904-824-2872
saintaugustinehistoricalsociety.org/oldest-house-museum-complex

The Oldest House Museum Complex is located across from the historic National Guard building in downtown St. Augustine. Admission includes a guided tour of Florida's Oldest House, a museum featuring a gallery of five centuries of American maps, a changing

Historic Buildings

exhibit gallery, a garden containing classic St. Augustine plants, and a museum store. The house is open from 10 a.m. to 5 p.m. daily, and tours run every half hour.

15 Pensacola Historic Village

120 Church St., Pensacola, Florida 32502; 850-595-5985
historicpensacola.org

Historic Pensacola is a neighborhood of 28 buildings that bring to life the city's more than 450-year history. The village is managed by the University of West Florida Historic Trust and is in downtown Pensacola. The district features charming homes, museums, art galleries, restaurants, and shops. Among the properties you will see are the T.T. Wentworth, Jr. Museum; Pensacola Children's Museum; Museum of Commerce; Museum of Industry; Old Christ Church; Tivoli High House; Dorr House; Julee Cottage, Fountain Park; and Colonial Archaeological Trail. Both guided and self-guided tours are available.

16 Seaside

Scenic Highway 30A, between Panama City Beach and Destin
seasidefl.com

Seaside is a planned community created in 1981 on what had been an 80-acre private family retreat near Seagrove Beach. The community is a pioneer of the concept now known as New Urbanism. Seaside has spurred the development of similar communities in Florida and elsewhere. It was also the setting for the movie *The Truman Show*. The town is designed for pedestrians. You can park your car and wander all over town on trails and sidewalks. The houses and other buildings are modern versions typical of Old Florida architecture with wide overhanging eaves, porches, and wood-frame construction.

17 Henry B. Plant Museum

401 W. Kennedy Blvd., Tampa, Florida 33606; 813-254-1891
plantmuseum.com

Plant Hall, the University of Tampa's central building, once housed the Tampa Bay Hotel. Built in 1891, the resort's Moorish minarets have long been an iconic symbol of Tampa. It was built by railroad magnate Henry B. Plant as a luxury resort hotel with more than 500 rooms and hosted such famous guests as Teddy Roosevelt and Stephen Crane. The Henry B. Plant Museum is inside and contains the actual furnishings enjoyed by the first guests to visit here, reflecting the opulence of turn-of-the-20th-century America and the vision of Henry B. Plant.

18 Vizcaya Museum & Gardens

3251 S. Miami Ave., Miami, Florida 33129; 305-250-9133
vizcaya.org

The Vizcaya Museum & Gardens is the former estate of James Deering of the Deering-McCormick International Harvester fortune. It is on Biscayne Bay in the Coconut Grove neighborhood of Miami. Built in the early 20th century, the estate's landscape and architecture were influenced by Italian Renaissance designs. Vizcaya was Deering's his winter residence from 1916 until his death in 1925. Recent hurricanes have damaged some of the open-air exhibits here, but it is in the process of restoration and is well worth a visit.

19 Ybor City Historic District

Ybor City Visitor Information Center, 1600 East 8th Avenue, Tampa, Florida 33605; 813-241-8838
ybor.org

You will enjoy walking the narrow brick streets of Ybor City and feeling its Old World charm. Known as Tampa's Latin Quarter for over a century, Ybor City is a National Historic Landmark District founded in 1886 by Don Vicente Martinez-Ybor when he moved his cigar factory from Key West to Tampa. Historic buildings have been preserved or converted to stylish offices, homes, and boutique hotels without sacrificing their historic character.

Some of the decór in the Ocean Drive District (photographed by lazyllama/Shutterstock)

Castillo de San Marcos (photographed by Kenneth Keifer/Shutterstock)

NATIVE AMERICANS WERE IN FLORIDA at least 12,000 years ago, but written records date back to when Juan Ponce de León arrived in 1513. Spain built St. Augustine and Pensacola in 1565 and governed Florida for most of the next 250 years until it became a territory of the United States in 1821 and a state in 1845. It was the third state to secede in the Civil War. Much of Florida heritage derives from the Old South, especially in north Florida. World War II spurred major economic development after its mild climate made the state a major military training center. Tourists began visiting, and many stayed. The population growth continues today.

FLORIDA HISTORY

1 The Barnacle Historic State Park

3485 Main Highway, Miami, Florida 33133; 305-442-6866
floridastateparks.org/parks-and-trails/barnacle-historic-state-park

This park is on Biscayne Bay in the historic Miami neighborhood of Coconut Grove. The Barnacle was the home of pioneer Ralph Middleton Munroe, who preserved the natural areas on his home site, cutting out only a narrow trail through the surrounding hammock. He built the home in 1891, and today's park looks like it did when Munroe lived here. He was a sailor and boat designer, and the park even contains replicas of two of his boats. The park is for simple relaxation: picnics, walking on the paths, or rocking in a chair on the front porch with views of the bay.

2 Castillo de San Marcos

1 S. Castillo Drive, St. Augustine, Florida 32084; 904-829-6506
nps.gov/casa

The Castillo dominates the waterfront and is the oldest structure in St. Augustine, completed by Spain in 1695. It sits on a 20-acre site and is the oldest 17th-century fort in North America. The fort has also been occupied by England, the Confederate States of America, and the United States. Native Americans, Minorcans, and African Americans also had roles in the fort's history. Your self-guided tour of the fort includes walking on and around the historic walls, reading the many exhibits, looking at the cannons, visiting the different rooms and learning about their functions, and reading about the history and culture of the various groups who are part of the fort's history. There are also guided tours.

3 Cracker Country Rural History Museum

4800 US 301 N, Tampa, Florida 33610; 813-627-4225
crackercountry.org

This attraction is open to the general public only during the Florida State Fair in February. A living-history museum located on the Florida State Fairgrounds in Tampa, Cracker Country features 13 buildings

Florida History

that were originally erected across the state between 1870 and 1912. The structures range from public buildings, like a general store and a train depot, to private spaces, such as pioneer homes. All have been decorated to display the lifestyle of the Florida pioneers, who were called Crackers. Costumed interpreters enhance this educational experience. Group tours can be arranged when the fair is not operating.

Fort Caroline National Memorial

12713 Fort Caroline Road, Jacksonville, Florida 32225; 904-641-7155
nps.gov/timu/learn/historyculture/foca.htm

This memorial, on a bluff on the south bank of the St. Johns River in Jacksonville, is dedicated to the French people who settled in Florida briefly in the 1500s. France and Spain struggled for control of Florida in the 16th century, and this fort was France's foothold in the New World. Exhibits explain the history of the fort and its role in various religious and territorial disputes, as well as the first interactions between the Europeans and Native Americans. The settlement at Fort Caroline did not survive beyond its first year. Spanish troops marched up from St. Augustine and destroyed it and most of its people. This site hosts the visitor center for the entire Timucuan Preserve, which includes Fort Caroline and Kingsley Plantation.

Fort Christmas Historical Park

1300 Fort Christmas Road, Christmas, Florida 32709; 407-254-9310
tinyurl.com/ftchristmas

The original Fort Christmas was built on Christmas Day 1837 during the Second Seminole Indian War. The fort you will visit is a full-scale replica that includes not only Seminole and pioneer artifacts but also weapons, clothing, tools, and other items. The park grounds also include some restored Florida Cracker houses and other buildings furnished with period pieces. The park has playgrounds, picnic areas, and a small museum and hosts several events during the year. Your visit will also include a video presentation of the history of the Seminole Indian Wars.

Fort Clinch State Park

2601 Atlantic Ave., Fernandina Beach, Florida 32034; 904-277-7274
floridastateparks.org/fortclinch

This state park combines Florida's natural beauty and a historic fort all in one setting. The 1,400-acre park has three miles of shoreline on the northern end of Amelia Island. The beaches on St. Marys Inlet and the Atlantic Ocean attract shellers, fishermen, and campers. The park includes miles of oak-canopied trails perfect for hiking or biking. A visit

to historic Fort Clinch includes talking to park staffers dressed as uniformed soldiers reenacting life during the Civil War. You can also explore the fort's many rooms and grounds. On the first weekend of every month, the fort has a staff of uniformed soldiers who demonstrate wartime skills such as carpentry, masonry, cooking, blacksmithing, and cannon firings.

7 Judah P. Benjamin Confederate Memorial at Gamble Plantation Historic State Park

3708 Patten Ave., Ellenton, Florida 34222; 941-723-4536
floridastateparks.org/parks-and-trails/judah-p-benjamin-confederate-memorial-gamble-plantation-historic-state-park

This pre–Civil War mansion, the only plantation home still standing in South Florida, was home to Major Robert Gamble, who owned an extensive sugar plantation. Historians believe this is where Confederate Secretary of State Judah P. Benjamin was sheltered after the end of the war, in the days leading up to his escape to England. You can take a guided tour of the home, which is furnished in mid-1800s style.

8 Kingsley Plantation

11676 Palmetto Avenue, Jacksonville, Florida 32226; 904-251-3537 or 904-251-3626
nps.gov/timu/learn/historyculture/kp.htm

Kingsley Plantation is located on Fort George Island on the Fort George River in Jacksonville. It is part of the Timucuan Preserve, which also encompasses the Fort Caroline National Memorial. The plantation was the estate of Zephaniah Kingsley, the owner of several plantations in Florida. On display at this park are the owner's house, probably built around 1798 and considered to be the oldest surviving plantation house in Florida. The park also includes the remains of 25 slave cabins that were still being used after the Civil War. The grounds of the park are open to the public daily, but tours of the plantation house are allowed only by reservation on a limited basis due to ongoing preservation efforts.

9 Koreshan State Park

3800 Corkscrew Road, Estero, Florida 33928; 239-992-0311
floridastateparks.org/parks-and-trails/koreshan-state-park

Florida has always had a reputation for attracting unusual people, and the Koreshan Unity was certainly unusual. This cult, who believed that the universe was contained within the Earth, settled in what is now Koreshan State Park. They prospered for years but died out because they all took a vow of chastity. The few elderly survivors donated their 305-acre site to the state. The grounds are loaded with natural Florida vegetation and include many gardens and exotic groves from when the Koreshans owned the land. The site includes 11 historic buildings with exhibits that explain the cult's beliefs. There are also several campsites spread throughout the wooded park.

10 Olustee Battlefield Historic State Park

5815 Battlefield Trail Road, Olustee, Florida 32087; 386-758-0400
floridastateparks.org/parks-and-trails/olustee-battlefield-historic-state-park

Although Florida escaped most of the major devastation caused in the South by the Civil War, it was the site of at least one significant battle. For five hours, 10,000 men, including the 54th Massachusetts Infantry regiment of the United States Colored Troops, waged a battle in the woods near Olustee. At the end of the day, 2,807 lives had been lost, and the Union troops had retreated to Jacksonville. The battlefield became the state's first historical site. You can use the picnic area and take a mile-long walk along an interpretative trail. The park has a visitor center with exhibits and artifacts from the battle, a reenactment of which is held every February.

11 Stephen Foster Folk Culture Center State Park

11016 Lillian Saunders Drive (US 41), White Springs, Florida 32096; 386-397-4331
floridastateparks.org/parks-and-trails/stephen-foster-folk-culture-center-state-park

This park honors the American composer Stephen Foster, who wrote what is now Florida's official song, "Old Folks at Home." This song made the Suwannee River famous, and the banks of the river are a logical place for this center. The museum contains exhibits about the composer's most famous songs, and many of them can be heard from the park's 97-bell carillon during the day. You can visit the gift shop and watch demonstrations of quilting, blacksmithing, and stained glass making. The park also has miles of trails and a campground. The Florida Folk Festival is held here every Memorial Day Weekend.

A pink flamingo at Zoo Tampa at Lowry Park (photographed by Nicole S Glass/Shutterstock)

FLORIDA ZOOS are home to animals native to the state but are also populated with many other species from all over the world. Some Florida animals you will see are panthers, alligators, snakes, foxes, frogs, and a wide variety of birds. Some zoos have elephants, giraffes, anteaters, bears, Gila monsters, and manatees. Many Florida zoos have up-close animal encounters that kids especially love, and in some cases you are allowed to feed certain animals.

ZOOS

1 Brevard Zoo

8225 N. Wickham Road, Melbourne, Florida 32940; 321-254-9453
brevardzoo.org

The small Brevard Zoo is one of the most popular zoos in Florida. You will see more than 195 species that include more than 900 different animals creatively housed on 22 acres of restored wetlands. The animals originate from Florida, Asia, Africa, Australia, and South America. One of the features of this zoo is that you can feed animals, such as the giraffes and birds, and you can ride a miniature train around the grounds through the animal's natural habitat. You can also purchase special tickets at the zoo that give you a unique adventure such as paddling a kayak or enjoying the petting zoo.

2 Catty Shack Ranch Wildlife Sanctuary

1860 Starratt Road, Jacksonville, Florida 32226; 904-757-3603
cattyshack.org

Catty Shack Ranch is a nonprofit wildlife sanctuary in Jacksonville. It has become one of the area's most popular visitor attractions. Their primary mission is to give endangered big cats a permanent home. They specialize in the rescue of exotic animals that are in danger. When an animal arrives at Catty Shack Ranch, it will have a loving home for the rest of its life. None of these animals are used for breeding, trading, selling, or buying. Animals currently living at Catty Shack Ranch include tigers, lions, leopards, lynx, foxes, and coatis. Even though the last two aren't cats, they have been given "honorary cat" status by the ranch.

3 Gatorland

14501 S. Orange Blossom Trail, Orlando, Florida 32837; 407-855-5496
gatorland.com

Gatorland has been thrilling visitors since 1949, a full 22 years before neighboring Walt Disney World opened its doors. It is a place for family fun, and the 110-acre park offers a true glimpse into the Old

Florida that is so quickly disappearing. You will see thousands of alligators (including some white ones), some crocodiles, a free-flight aviary, and several animal shows. For an extra charge, you can even soar above the hungry gators on a zip line.

4 Jacksonville Zoo and Gardens

370 Zoo Pkwy., Jacksonville, Florida 32218; 904-757-4463
jacksonvillezoo.org

This zoo is more than 100 years old and is located on 89 acres on the shore of Trout River, north of downtown Jacksonville. The zoo is organized by natural exhibits, including River Valley Aviary, African Forest, Stingray Bay, Wild Florida, Giraffe Overlook, and Range of the Jaguar. For the kids, there is also the Play Park and Splash Ground and the ability to pet the stingrays in Stingray Bay. The Gardens at Trout River Plaza is a large botanical garden where facilities can be rented for special events. Kids also love feeding the lorikeets at Australian Adventure.

5 Lion Country Safari

2003 Lion Country Safari Road, Loxahatchee, Florida 33470; 561-793-1084
lioncountrysafari.com

Lion Country Safari is an unusual amusement park where you drive your own car through the grounds. You can spend an entire day driving among the more than 1,000 animals. The attraction also has rides and a water-spray feature for the kids, animal-feeding experiences, a restaurant, shops, a campground, and a lot more. Some of the animals you will see include tortoises, tapirs, alpacas, impalas, ostriches, water buffaloes, lions, Ankole-Watusi cattle, rhinos, zebras, and chimpanzees. A sister attraction, Safari World, is nearby that costs less and lets you walk through animal exhibits.

6 Zoo Tampa at Lowry Park

1101 W. Sligh Ave., Tampa, Florida 33604; 813-935-8552
zootampa.org

This zoo is one of the most popular in Florida, with over 1 million annual visitors. The zoo occupies 56 acres of naturalistic animal exhibits in a tropical garden setting and has many up-close animal encounters that both kids and adults enjoy. The zoo pays special attention to endangered species from world climates similar to that of the Tampa Bay area. There are park zones devoted to Asia, Africa, Australia, and Florida. More than 1,300 animals make their home in the zoo. Another interesting feature is the Manatee Critical Care Center, the only one of its kind in Florida. Zoo guests can have the experience of watching through windows while the staff treat injured and orphaned manatees.

Zoos

7 Naples Zoo at Caribbean Gardens

1590 Goodlette-Frank Road, Naples, Florida 34102; 239-262-5409
napleszoo.org

This zoo was established in 1919 when Naples was still a small settlement on the southwestern frontier of Florida. It was originally established as a botanical garden, which explains its full name. Many of the more than 3,000 plants from the original gardens are still thriving today. Animals live in habitats designed to enhance their freedom and natural surroundings. You will see gators, anteaters, bears, cheetahs, snakes, foxes, frogs, gibbons, and even a honey badger that the children love to interact with (he's behind very strong glass).

8 St. Augustine Alligator Farm Zoological Park

999 Anastasia Blvd., St. Augustine, Florida 32080; 904-824-3337
alligatorfarm.com

This is one of several Florida tourist attractions on the National Register of Historic Places. It was founded in 1893 and has entertained and educated millions of people about alligators. This zoo also has hundreds of other species, including birds, lemurs, snakes, turtles, and even porcupines and albino alligators. The attraction also has a zip line where you can soar over the gators as you imagine them licking their chops.

9 Zoo World

9008 Front Beach Road, Panama City Beach, Florida 32407; 850-230-1243
zooworldpcb.com

The full name of this attraction is Zoo World Zoological and Botanical Conservatory. The zoo specializes in conservation and has over 260 animals with numerous exhibits, programs, and performances in a tropical setting. This is an interactive attraction where you can have up-close experiences with sloths, giraffes, lemurs, alligators, and birds. These encounters usually include holding and petting the animal. Most of the encounters cost an additional fee. There are also various dispensers around the zoo where you can buy food to feed the animals.

St. Augustine Alligator Farm Zoological Park (photographed by Bob Pool/Shutterstock)

Lionesses at Busch Gardens In Tampa (photographed by Raymond Louis RS/Shutterstock)

DOES YOUR PERFECT DAY include a family visit to a giant theme park, or would you rather go to a smaller and less expensive attraction? No matter your preference, there are hundreds if not thousands of fun getaways in Florida. Orlando and Central Florida are home to some of the largest theme parks in the world. Smaller attractions are scattered across the state. From water parks to roller coasters to giant Ferris wheels, it can be found in Florida.

AMUSEMENT AND THEME PARKS

1 Busch Gardens

10165 N. McKinley Drive, Tampa, Florida 33612; 813-884-4386
buschgardens.com/tampa

You will never get bored at Busch Gardens in Tampa. It is a 335-acre animal-themed park that contains nine roller coasters, two water rides, plus other rides and animal attractions. The park is also adjacent to a sister water park, Adventure Island. Busch Gardens has several themed areas and attractions, such as Morocco, Congo, Nairobi, Edge of Africa, and Egypt. Some are walk-through exhibits where you can observe animals in their natural habitat. Bird Gardens is a free-flight aviary where more than 500 tropical birds from all over the world make their homes. You can also hand-feed a kangaroo and see crocodiles, meerkats, lions, hyenas, and hippos.

2 Daytona International Speedway

1801 W. International Speedway Blvd., Daytona Beach, Florida 32114; 800-748-7467
daytonainternationalspeedway.com

This famous racetrack features several events during the year, such as the Daytona 500, the Rolex 24, and many more. If you are in Daytona at times other than race days, the speedway offers tours on a first-come, first-served basis. Drive through the main entrance and follow the signs to the tours. There are three basic tour types: Speedway, All-Access, and VIP. The tours range in time from 30 minutes for the Speedway to 90 minutes for the All-Access, and 3 hours for the VIP. Prices increase as tour time increases. These are tram tours, and after the tour you can visit the Motorsports Hall of Fame of America. You will see all kinds of stock cars, sports cars, and motorcycles.

3 Dinosaur World

5145 Harvey Tew Road, Plant City, Florida 33565; 813-717-9865
dinosaurworld.com/florida

Nobody seems to know for sure why kids are so crazy about dinosaurs, but a visit to this place will convince you they are. You will have a chance to wander around hundreds of replicas of the giant reptiles, displayed in their true size. *Tyrannosaurus rex* is there, of course, along with even scarier creatures you might never have heard of. You can uncover a 27-foot dinosaur skeleton at the Bone Yard and pretend you are an paleontologist at the Fossil Dig. The Exploration Cave Show lets you interact with a paleontologist on a tour through a cave, a dig site, and a workstation. There is also a separate museum, a gift shop, and a playground, as well as plenty of free parking.

4 Disney Springs

1486 E. Buena Vista Drive, Orlando, Florida 32830; 407-939-6244
disneysprings.com

You will have no trouble at all spending an enjoyable day or two at Disney Springs, an outdoor shopping, dining, and entertainment complex at Walt Disney World Resort. The original complex opened in 1975 and has been expanded and renamed over the years. Disney Springs has a fictional history that says it was settled in the 1800s by a cattle rancher. The complex has four separately themed areas, each reflecting a different time in the fictional history of the town. Each area has an architectural style typical of its period. Admission is free. Buses and water taxis operated by Disney Transport provide transportation between Disney Springs and other areas of Walt Disney World Resort.

5 Epcot

Walt Disney World Resort, 200 Epcot Center Drive, Orlando, Florida 32821;
407-939-5277
disneyworld.disney.go.com/destinations/epcot

Epcot is one of the four theme parks at Walt Disney World Resort. It celebrates human achievement in technology and features international culture zones. It is divided into two main areas: Future World and World Showcase. Future World has several pavilions that contain exhibits and rides exhibiting innovative technology. These include Spaceship Earth, Innoventions, Mission: Space, Test Track, The Seas with Nemo & Friends, The Land, Imagination!, and a seasonal festival center. The World Showcase resembles a permanent World's Fair with 11 themed pavilions, each representing a specific country. The countries are Canada, China, France, Germany, Italy, Japan, Mexico, Morocco, Norway, the United Kingdom, and the USA. Each pavilion has themed architecture along with shops and restaurants typical of the country's culture and cuisine.

**6, 8, 9
7, 10**

6 Fun Spot America

5700 Fun Spot Way, Orlando, Florida 32819; 407-363-3867
fun-spot.com

Fun Spot America is located on the busy International Drive entertainment corridor in Orlando. It has four go-kart tracks and two roller coasters, including Florida's only wooden coaster. The park also has five thrill rides, including the world's second-tallest SkyCoaster at 250 feet. In this ride, one to three riders are winched to the top of a tall launch arch and then suddenly dropped. They swing back and forth on a tether until finally coming to rest, somewhat like in bungee jumping.

7 Legoland Florida Resort

1 Legoland Way, Winter Haven, Florida 33884; 888-690-5346
legoland.com/florida

The 150-acre Legoland Florida Resort is built on the former Cypress Gardens theme park and preserves many reminders of that property's history, such as a banyan tree that was planted as a seedling in 1939. Legoland has more than 50 rides and attractions, along with shows, shops, restaurants, and a water park, all based on Lego brands and characters. The resort also has two hotels: the Legoland Hotel with 152 rooms, and the Legoland Beach Retreat with 166 rooms in 83 freestanding bungalows designed to look like giant Lego sets. The new Legoland Pirate Island Hotel is scheduled to open in spring 2020. Daily events at the park feature a water-ski show that includes humans and costumed Lego characters like Captain Brickbeard. Fun things for the kids to do include building a Lego car and testing it on a digitally timed track.

8 ICON Park

8401 International Drive, #100, Orlando, Florida 32819; 407-601-7907
iconparkorlando.com

ICON Orlando, formerly known as the Orlando Eye before being rebranded in 2018, is a 400-foot tall observation wheel that can be seen for miles and is illuminated at night by colored lights. The wheel is part of a complex of shops, restaurants, and other attractions on International Drive. The owners call it an observation wheel rather than a Ferris wheel because the capsule in which you ride is stabilized and doesn't swing back and forth. The wheel has 30 air-conditioned passenger capsules, each with a capacity of up to 15 people. The view from each carriage is spectacular, and the ride takes about 22 minutes. You can see area hotels, SeaWorld, Universal Orlando, and downtown Orlando. At the top you can see Walt Disney World, including Space Mountain, Spaceship Earth, and the Contemporary hotel. On clear days you might even see the Atlantic Ocean, more than 50 miles east.

9 SeaWorld

7007 Sea World Drive, Orlando, Florida 32821; 407-545-5550
seaworld.com/orlando

At SeaWorld Orlando, dolphins, manta rays, sea lions, and other marine creatures are featured throughout, and many perform in shows. You can get close to many of the animals and interact with them. The park features three roller coasters: Kraken (a floorless coaster), Manta (a coaster designed to mimic the movement of a manta ray), and Mako (named for one of the fastest sharks). It is also home to the original Journey to Atlantis water ride. On Electric Ocean nights (select nights May 24–September 1), nighttime shows feature fireworks; music; and performances by sea lions, otters, or dolphins.

10 Spook Hill

Fifth Street, adjacent to Spook Hill Elementary School on Dr. J. A. Wiltshire Ave.,
Lake Wales, Florida 33853
florida-backroads-travel.com/spook-hill.html

Spook Hill is a free optical illusion attraction that has been entertaining people for a long time. The illusion happens when you park your car at the bottom of the hill and put it in neutral. The car appears to be coasting slowly up the hill, defying gravity. A white line has been painted on the street so you know where to park your car. If all goes as expected, your car will start its self-powered trip up the hill. Although there are several folk legends about why this happens, the truth is that the lay of the land and growth pattern of the trees make it look like up is down and vice versa. It doesn't matter to you because you still experience that mystical feeling of beating gravity at its own game.

11 Universal Orlando Resort

6000 Universal Blvd., Orlando, Florida 32819; 407-363-8000
universalorlando.com

Universal Orlando is the second-largest resort in Orlando, surpassed only by Walt Disney World. It consists of two theme parks: Universal Studios Florida and Universal's Islands of Adventure. It also includes a water park called Volcano Bay, a nighttime entertainment complex called Universal CityWalk, and six hotels. The theme parks are each unique in their own way. Universal Studios Florida is made up of themed areas and attractions based on pop culture icons, TV, and movies. The eight themed areas are designed to make you feel like you are on a movie set. Universal's Islands of Adventure consists of seven distinct simulated islands, each themed to various adventures. The Wizarding World of Harry Potter is one of the most popular attractions here. Universal CityWalk is located at the entrance, and visitors travel on moving covered walkways to either of the two main theme parks.

12 Walt Disney World Resort

Walt Disney World Resort, Orlando, Florida 32830; 407-939-5277
disneyworld.disney.go.com

Walt Disney World Resort is the most-visited vacation resort in the world, covering more than 25,000 acres and featuring six theme parks (Magic Kingdom, Epcot, Disney's Hollywood Studios, and Animal Kingdom, Toy Story Land, and the newest attraction, Star Wars: Galaxy's Edge), two water parks (Typhoon Lagoon and Blizzard Beach), more than 25 themed resort hotels, four golf courses, an RV park, and many entertainment and shopping venues, including Disney Springs. The resort has an annual attendance of more than 52 million. There are so many things to see and do that one could easily spend a month and not see it all. There are always special events under way, and Disney offers ticket packages to include one or more theme parks for 1–10 days. Their website is an indispensable resource to see what's currently available.

13 Weeki Wachee Springs State Park

6131 Commercial Way, Spring Hill, Florida 34606; 352-592-5656
weekiwachee.com

Weeki Wachee Springs and its mermaid show was one of Florida's earliest pre-Disney attractions and is now part of the Florida state park system. Mermaid shows are still being held daily, and Buccaneer Bay, a water park with a four waterslides, has been open for nearly 40 years. Don't be surprised if you see other Florida natives swimming with the mermaids. These natives include turtles, fish, manatees, otters, and even an occasional gator. You can also rent inner tubes or kayaks and drift down the river.

A flower at Fairchild Tropical Botanical Garden (photographed by Keith Michael Taylor/Shutterstock)

FLORIDA'S MILD TO TROPICAL CLIMATE makes it ideal for growing a large variety of plants. The huge population explosion in recent state history makes these botanical gardens even more attractive. They are peaceful oases that provide refuge and quiet among the busy state of Florida.

GARDENS, FLOWERS, AND ARBORETUMS

1 Bonnet House Museum & Gardens

900 N. Birch Road, Fort Lauderdale, Florida 33304; 954-563-5393
bonnethouse.org

Bonnet House is a 35-acre estate on the heavily developed Fort Lauderdale Beach oceanfront and is listed on the National Register of Historic Places. The main house is full of furniture and art from the collections of the families who lived there over the years. The grounds include one of the few remaining native barrier island habitats in South Florida. Five different ecosystems are represented, and complementing the natural flora is a desert garden composed of arid plants, a hibiscus garden, and a courtyard planted with tropical vegetation. There are many orchids in this garden, and various specimens are on view at the Orchid Display House. Migratory birds find refuge at Bonnet House, and occasionally even manatees will come into the estate's Boathouse Canal.

2 Fairchild Tropical Botanic Garden

10901 Old Cutler Road, Coral Gables, Florida 33156; 305-667-1651
fairchildgarden.org

This 83-acre garden is considered to be one of the world's best tropical botanic gardens. It has extensive collections of rare tropical plants and has one of the largest collections of palms in the world. You will become immersed in tropical beauty as you walk along the many paths and enjoy the displays. It is much more than a tourist attraction. It is one of the leading conservation and educational facilities in the world. Fairchild is heavily supported by the community with over 45,000 members and 1,200 volunteers who work in the gardens. And you'll definitely see orchids: Fairchild is the home of the American Orchid Society.

3 Leu Gardens

1920 N. Forest Ave., Orlando, Florida 32803; 407-246-2620
leugardens.org

The Harry P. Leu Gardens are located in north Orlando on 50 acres of some of the most beautiful botanical gardens in Florida. It has been a popular attraction since 1961, when it was donated to the city by the Leu family. The property is divided into more than 10 garden areas connected by sidewalks, so you can enjoy self-guided tours. The variety of plants is amazing and includes bananas, bromeliads, birds of paradise, cactus, bamboo, herbs, citrus and vegetables. Some of their vegetable harvest goes to local food banks, and some is used in cooking classes that are held on the property in the Garden House.

4 Marie Selby Botanical Gardens

900 S. Palm Ave., Sarasota, Florida 34236; 941-366-5731
selby.org

This small botanical garden is only 15 acres, with 9 acres of display gardens. It is unique, however, as the only botanical garden in the world that is dedicated to epiphytes, or plants that grow on the surface of other plants. Marie Selby also focuses on orchids and bromeliads. The gardens feature more than 20,000 living plants, including 5,500 orchids, 3,500 bromeliads, and 1,600 other plants. There are also banyans, bamboo, live oaks, palms, mangoes, succulents, wildflowers, cycads, a butterfly garden, a scent garden, and an interactive children's rainforest garden. The gardens are located on the former estate of Marie and William Selby of the Texaco Oil Company.

5 Morikami Museum and Japanese Gardens

4000 Morikami Park Road, Delray Beach, Florida 33446; 561-495-0233
morikami.org

The Morikami Museum and Japanese Gardens has Japanese cultural exhibits that educate and inspire visitors. The history of this attraction has its roots in the Yamato Colony, a small community of Japanese pioneers who lived near Boca Raton and Delray Beach in the early 1900s. The museum building is modeled after a Japanese villa and has exhibition rooms surrounding an open courtyard with a dry garden of gravel, pebbles, and small boulders. The building also has a 225-seat theater and an authentic tea house and a café. The 16-acre grounds around the museum include Japanese gardens with walking paths, rest areas, and a large bonsai collection. The entire park contains 200 acres and has nature trails, pine forests, and picnic areas.

Gardens, Flowers,

6 Naples Botanical Garden

4820 Bayshore Drive, Naples, Florida 34112; 239-643-7275
naplesgarden.org

This garden calls itself the "Gardens with Latitude" because they focus on collections and habitats representative of plants that exist between the latitudes of 26° N and 26° S. The garden features plants from all over the world that grow within this zone. The exhibits are arranged in several gardens that include Asian, Brazilian, Caribbean, Children's, Florida, and Water. The Chabraja Visitor Center contains Kathryn's Garden, Irma's Garden (chosen for captivating colors), and LaGrippe Orchid Garden. There is also a 90-acre nature preserve with several native Florida habitats where you can see eagles, otters, tree frogs, and gopher tortoises in their natural settings.

7 Sunken Gardens

1825 Fourth St. N, St. Petersburg, Florida 33704; 727-551-3102
stpete.org/attractions/sunken_gardens

Sunken Gardens is a century-old botanical garden in the middle of busy urban St. Petersburg. You will enjoy winding paths surrounded by exotic plants from all regions of the world. You can also sign up for garden tours, horticultural programs, and special events. Your tour will take you past cascading waterfalls, demonstration gardens, and more than 50,000 tropical plants and flowers. Some recent special event topics included Frogs and Toads in the Garden, Colorful Caladiums!, and Easy Natives and Wildflowers.

When you check into the gardens you will be provided with a map that gives you details on the various plants. Parking is free.

Leu Gardens (photographed by RHMeeks/Shutterstock)

Sloppy Joe's in Key West (photographed by Alfred Wekelo/Shutterstock)

RELIABLE SOURCES CLAIM that Florida has about 40,000 restaurants, wineries, bars, diners, and other establishments to enjoy good spirits and good times. We scratch the surface here with some of the oldest and most popular establishments. You can enjoy a wide variety of food, drinks, and entertainment at these places.

GOOD SPIRITS AND GOOD TIMES

1 Alabama Jack's

58000 Card Sound Road, Key Largo, Florida 33037; 305-248-8741
facebook.com/pages/alabama-jacks-key-largo-florida/179175785438865

When you are traveling to the Florida Keys down US 1, there are only two ways to get there. One is to turn left on Card Sound Road after leaving Homestead. This takes you through mangrove swamps to a bridge that crosses Card Sound onto north Key Largo. Alabama Jack's is on the right side of the road just before the bridge. It is a typical old waterfront restaurant. There is a nice bar inside, and plenty of indoor and outdoor seating. They have good seafood, including grouper sandwiches, a grilled dolphin platter, crab cake sandwiches, and conch fritters. You don't go here as much for the food as for the experience. The bar serves great margaritas and there are lots of beer, wine, and liquor choices. They often have live music in the Jimmy Buffett style.

2 Bern's Steak House

1208 S. Howard Ave., Tampa, Florida 33606; 813-251-2421
bernssteakhouse.com

When I lived in Tampa, I always took my out-of-town visitors to Bern's. It is one of the earliest examples of farm-to-table restaurants in Florida. In Bern's case, they own their own farm, so they know exactly what they are serving. They are famous for their perfectly aged steaks. My personal favorite is their 6-ounce filet mignon. They have one of the largest wine collections in the world, and guests are invited to take a tour of the huge wine cellar and kitchen. They are well worth visiting. Bern's also has an internationally famous dessert room. Although I am usually not a dessert person, I always visit this room and usually select a King Midas spiced carrot cake to finish off my meal. These features have made Bern's a local favorite since 1956.

3

Cap's Place Island Restaurant

(Dock Location) 2765 NE 28th Court, Lighthouse Point, Florida 33064; 954-941-0418
capsplace.com

Historic Cap's Place was established in 1928 and is an Old Florida icon
that should be visited at least once by everyone interested in Florida
history. It is on the National Register of Historic Places. People go to
Cap's for the ambience. Many famous visitors have dined and imbibed
here, including Joe DiMaggio, Jack Dempsey, and Myrna Loy. Cap's is on
the tip of a residential peninsula. You get there by a 5-minute boat ride
that operates out of Lighthouse Point marina. The walls of the restaurant are filled with photos and newspaper clippings of the old days.
Cap's overlooks the water with views of yachts, mansions, and shoreline
mangroves. The menu specializes in fresh fish, scallops, crab cakes,
shrimp dishes, and lobster. They also have hearts of palm salad (swamp
cabbage), and Key lime pie.

4

The Chattaway

358 22nd Ave. S, St. Petersburg, Florida 33705; 727-823-1594
thechattaway.com

This Old Florida establishment has been serving casual diners in
St. Petersburg since 1951. It features outdoor dining and is a favorite
of the locals. Tourists have a bit harder time finding it because it is a
little south of the downtown district of marinas and museums. A dis-
tinctive feature of the decor is the ubiquitous claw-foot bathtubs, which
are used as planters for exotic flowers and tropical plants. The most
famous dish here is the 7-ounce hamburger loaded with everything
you want and named the Chattaburger. There are other sandwiches,
seafood entrées, salads, and soups, as well, and they also serve beer
and wine.

5

Clark's Fish Camp

12903 Hood Landing Road, Jacksonville, Florida 32258; 904-268-3474
clarksfishcamp.net

You will not see another restaurant in Florida quite like Clark's Fish
Camp. It has been entertaining people with good food and atmosphere
for decades. The food is good, but the interior is what amazes visitors. It
is stuffed with what may be one of the country's largest private taxidermy collections. You will be dining next to lifelike mounted panthers,
lions, deer, fish, birds, and more. Seafood is the big thing on the menu,
and you can find just about anything from the sea you might want. Enjoy
oysters, catfish, trout, frog legs, and more. If you are a landlubber, you
can choose from a wide selection of beef offerings. Clark's also has a full

bar. In addition to the taxidermy collection, you may be able to see an alligator feeding. The gator, Lilly, lives in an aquarium, where people waiting for a table can watch her lying there minding her own business.

6 Columbia Restaurant

2117 E. Seventh Ave., Tampa, Florida 33605; 813-248-4961
columbiarestaurant.com

My first job after graduating from college was in Tampa. My boss took me and my wife to the Columbia, and it was one of the most fantastic experiences I have ever had. Taking up an entire Ybor City block, it is one of the largest Spanish restaurants in the world, seating 1,700 in 15 dining rooms. The interior architecture is breathtaking. The oldest restaurant in Florida, Columbia was founded in 1905 by a Cuban immigrant, Casimiro Hernandez Sr., and is still operated by his descendants. The food is delicious Spanish and Cuban cuisine, and the sangria and other drinks are great. They have a 50,000-bottle wine inventory. The entertainment is also fabulous, featuring a world-class flamenco show. The Columbia's success has led to several other operations around Florida featuring the name, but this location is the original and, in my opinion, the best.

7 Henscratch Farms Vineyard and Winery

980 Henscratch Road, Lake Placid, Florida 33852; 863-699-2060
henscratchfarms.com

Henscratch Farms Vineyards and Winery is unique in that it is also a small working farm. Two hundred hens have free range under the canopy of the vineyard. Several breeds of laying hens wander the property, but one makes me think of the children's author Dr. Seuss. The Aracaunas lay large green eggs. Remember the silly book about green eggs and ham? The winery's small country store is built in the old-fashioned Florida Cracker style. Inside you will find many types of wine, jams, jellies, sauces, and syrups. Products vary with the harvest season. Strawberry preserves, blueberry dressing, and jams and jellies are displayed on the tasting counter, so you can try a sample and sip some wine. They also sell eggs and raw honey from their own hives.

8 High Tides at Snack Jack

2805 S. Oceanshore Blvd., Flagler Beach, Florida 32136; 386-439-3344
snackjacks.com

Snack Jack has been at this beachfront location since 1947. It is directly on the ocean, and every booth or table has a view of the rolling surf. There is also outside dining. The menu of course is loaded with seafood dishes, including platters, conch fritters, tacos, sandwiches, and salads. The kitchen knows how to steam, grill, blacken, and prepare all kinds of food the way you like, including the good old frying method. The minute you walk inside the rambling rustic building, you will feel like you've been transported to a surfing museum. The walls and ceilings are festooned with all kinds of interesting objects, including surf-boards. The main dining room also has a small bar where you can eat or just have a drink. Don't dress up to go to Snack Jack. T-shirt, shorts, and flip-flops are always in style here.

9 Joe's Stone Crab

11 Washington Ave., Miami Beach, Florida 33139; 305-673-0365
joesstonecrab.com

When I lived on my boat in Miami Beach, a favorite evening tradition was a stroll to nearby Joe's Stone Crab for drinks and dinner. The restaurant was opened in 1913 by Joe Weiss. After all these years, Joe's is still the top buyer of Florida stone crab claws, their most famous dish. Joe's is frequented by the rich and famous, but I used to go there, so you can too. The servers are professionals, and many of their fathers and grandfathers also worked at Joe's. The maître d' is king. They take no reservations, so you approach him and give him your name and the size of your party. You might give him a tip at this point, and I don't mean "buy low and sell high." Then you will wait, but the wait is a lot of fun, especially at the bar. Although there are many other items on the menu, if you come for stone crabs, remember they are seasonal and must be cooked the day they are caught. The best time to go is during the season, from October 15 to May 15. Prices vary by harvest and amount.

10 Lakeridge Winery & Vineyards

19239 US 27 N, Clermont, Florida 34715; 800-768-9463
lakeridgewinery.com

This winery has become a popular Orlando-area attraction. The beautiful main building and vineyards are on a 127-acre estate in the hilly country about 25 miles west of Orlando. The vineyard takes up 77 acres and includes Florida hybrid bunch grapes and varieties of musca-dines. The winery has a large tasting room and an attractive gift shop.

Several types of wine are sold under the Lakeridge brands. In addition to the wines, the gift shop sells gourmet foods, cheeses, crackers, sauces, and wine accessories. There are probably more events held at this establishment than at any other Florida winery. All year long, there are art and craft shows, jazz concerts, harvest festivals, grape-stomping events, vintage car shows, and vintage music events. Complimentary tours and wine tastings are offered daily.

11 Mai-Kai Restaurant

3599 N. Federal Hwy., Fort Lauderdale, Florida 33308; 954-563-3272
maikai.com

Mai-Kai is a Polynesian-themed restaurant and nightclub that opened in 1956 and is on the National Register of Historic Places. When you step inside, you feel like you are in a tropical place on some South Sea island. The extensive menu includes duck, beef, chicken, pork, seafood, and vegetarian selections. All food is prepared with Asian spices using Asian cooking techniques. The drinks are huge, and it only takes one to get you in the mood for the Polynesian stage show you will enjoy after dinner. Dancers show their stuff to fantastic drum beats with lots of fiery torches. Dress up a little bit—no T-shirts and baggy shorts. No coat and tie required, but wear a shirt with a collar and some nice shorts or slacks.

12 San Sebastian Winery

157 King St., St. Augustine, Florida 32084; 904-826-1594
sansebastianwinery.com

This winery has been in business since 1996 and is the second-largest winery in Florida. Over 160,000 visitors a year come to taste wine and tour the 18,0000-square-foot facility, which has a gourmet gift shop and a storage capacity of 40,000 gallons of wine. Besides the wines, you can purchase domestic and imported beers, as well as appetizers. Native varieties of red 'Noble' and bronze 'Carlos' and 'Welder' muscadines are grown for the winery by Lakeridge Winery Estate and Prosperity Vineyards. There is an open-air deck on the second floor where you can enjoy your wine and snacks while listening to music. The view of St. Augustine is wonderful from the deck, and music is provided every weekend.

13 Schnebly Redland's Winery

30205 SW 217th Ave., Homestead, Florida 33030; 305-242-1224
schneblywinery.com

Schnebly Redland's Winery is noted not just for its exotic wine but also for its entertaining and comfortable venue. The winery makes delicious wines out of all kinds of tropical fruits. The Redland is a large agricultural area that gets its name from the red clay soil that dominates the area. Exotic plants and vegetables that will not grow anywhere else in the United States thrive in the soil here. The winery's 96 acres of tropical fruits include carambola, mango, lychee, guava, passion fruit, and gourmet vegetables. The buildings and grounds are beautifully maintained, and there are a couple of fountains and waterfalls located among the lush tropical plantings that surround the building. The retail store and wine-tasting areas are up front.

14 Sloppy Joe's

201 Duval St., Key West, Florida 33040; 305-294-5717
sloppyjoes.com

Sloppy Joe's Bar has long been a part of the quirky nature of Key West. It was a favorite hangout of Ernest Hemingway, who lived in Key West for many years. People visit the bar mainly for its historic atmosphere, but it also serves good drinks and decent food, including salads and pizza. Millions of locals and visitors have come here since it first went into business under another name in the 1930s.

Saturn V Engines, Kennedy Space Center (photographed by Samot/Shutterstock)

FLORIDA'S MODERN HISTORY began first with railroads, then airplanes, and finally rockets. After the Civil War, water routes were the main form of transportation in the state. Railroads made the development of Florida possible by increasing export routes for its agricultural products, and enabling tourists to come down from the north. Aviation followed during World Wars I and II, and the modern space program began in Florida at Cape Canaveral with the launch of *Bumper 8* in 1950. Federal, state, and local governments, along with private individuals, have done a great job preserving the memories and artifacts of these eras.

ROCKETS, AIRPLANES, AND RAILROADS

1 Aerospace Discovery at the Florida Air Museum

4175 Medulla Road, Lakeland, Florida 33811; 863-904-6833
flysnf.org

Designated as Florida's "Official Aviation Museum and Education Center," this museum is housed in a building on the campus of the Sun 'n Fun Fly-In and Expo at Lakeland Linder Regional Airport. The museum features a display of one-of-a-kind designs, classics, ultralights, antiques, and war planes. In addition to aircraft, there is a large collection of aircraft engines from World War I to the present day. Aerospace Discovery at the Florida Air Museum continues to grow and is becoming a showcase for Florida's aviation history through exhibits, restoration and preservation, education, and outreach so that all ages may share the passion of flight.

2 Air Force Armament Museum

100 Museum Drive, Eglin Air Force Base, Florida 32542; 850-882-4062
afarmamentmuseum.com

The museum showcases the armament of aviation warfare from World War I all the way to today's high-technology planes, guns, and bombs. They have a large collection of weapons and cockpit simulators that will keep an aviation buff busy for hours. As you drive onto the museum property, you will see many aircraft on display, including the SR-71 Blackbird, the fastest air-breathing plane ever built. There are other planes from World War II, the Korean War, the Vietnam War, and the Gulf War eras. There are four more aircraft inside the museum building itself, as well as a huge variety of bombs, missiles, and rockets.

3 Air Force Space & Missile Museum

Launch Complex 26, Kennedy Space Center Visitor Complex; 855-433-4210
afspacemuseum.org

The public can visit this museum only by special bus tour from the Kennedy Space Center Visitor Complex. The tour takes 3 hours and stops at several other historic sites at Cape Canaveral Air Force Station. The museum includes many exhibits about the history of rocketry and space flight, and the grounds encompass two adjoining launch complexes: 26 and 5/6. Launch Complex 26 is the site of the first successful launch of an American satellite, *Explorer I,* in 1958. From 1957 until its deactivation in 1963, Launch Complex 26 conducted 36 launches. These launches included the three primates that led the way for manned space flights. Launch Complex 5/6 was the launch site for the earliest Project Mercury missions. It was from Pad 5 in 1961 that Alan Shepard and Gus Grissom were launched into space.

4 Central Florida Railroad Museum

101 S. Boyd St., Winter Garden, Florida 34787; 407-656-0559
cfrhs.org/museum

This small museum is managed by the Central Florida Railway Historical Society and focuses on the railroads of Central Florida. Among items exhibited are historical photographs, including an extensive collection of Tavares & Gulf Railroad photographs from its early steam era until its last run. You will also see lanterns, locks, old telephones, telegraphs, signs, stoves, tools, furniture, timetables, dining car table ware, ticket punches, lamps, uniforms, locomotive bells and whistles, a 1938 Fairmont motorcar, and a velocipede hand car. A caboose is on display outside the museum, along with a three-head interlocking signal from a former junction in Plant City, a set of narrow-gauge wheels, and several switch stands and crossing signals.

5 Fantasy of Flight

1400 Broadway Blvd. SE, Polk City, Florida 33868; 863-984-3500
fantasyofflight.com

You will be amazed at what you see and experience here. Aviation pioneer Kermit Weeks opened Fantasy of Flight in 1995 to share his love for aviation and aircraft. It is home to the world's largest private collection of vintage aircraft. There are more than 140 civilian and military planes, and many are air-worthy. A portion of the collection is always on display. There are also themed immersion experiences, flight simulators, interactive exhibits, and tram tours. It is a great place to learn about aviation history. One good way to see the place is by taking a guided tour. It is also useful to check out Fantasy of Flight's Facebook page and that of Kermit Weeks to see what is currently happening. Fantasy of Flight even has its own airfield, shown on the charts as "Orlampa," so named because it is about halfway between Orlando and Tampa.

6 Florida Railroad Museum

12210 83rd St. E, Parrish, Florida 34219; 941-776-0906
frrm.org

It you love trains, there is a lot to love here. This is one of three official state railroad museums in Florida. The museum has a large collection of rolling stock, including 13 locomotives; 9 passenger cars, including Pullmans; 6 cabooses; and various kinds of freight cars. Some of the locomotives and cars are in service, and the others are for display only. The ticket office and gift shop are open Wednesday–Sunday, and 13-mile train rides take place on most Saturdays and Sundays, departing at 11 a.m. and 2 p.m. The locomotive pulls cars consisting of open-window coaches, a covered gondola, and an air-conditioned coach.

7 Kennedy Space Center Visitor Complex

Space Commerce Way, Merritt Island, FL 32953; 855-433-4210
kennedyspacecenter.com

Kennedy Space Center is where the United States began its journey into space and where that journey continues to this day. There is so much to see and do here that at least one day should be set aside to make your visit worthwhile. The website lets you plan your trip in advance and choose your own itinerary based on the age of any children in your party and how many days you have to spend. The complex features exhibits and displays, historic spacecraft and memorabilia, shows, an IMAX theater, and a range of bus tours of the spaceport. The Space Shuttle *Atlantis* exhibit is home to the orbiter of the same name, and the Shuttle Launch Experience is a simulated trip into space. The complex also has daily presentations from a veteran NASA astronaut. A bus tour, included with admission, encompasses the separate Apollo/Saturn V Center. You will be among the approximately 1.5 million annual visitors who enjoy the complex.

8 Murder Mystery Dinner Train

Colonial Station, 2805 Colonial Blvd., Fort Myers, Florida 33966; 239-275-8487
semgulf.com

Have you ever wanted to go to a murder mystery dinner? Have you
ever wanted to ride on a train? Here is your chance to do both.
Enjoy a five-course dinner while watching a mystery play—usually a comedy—and helping to solve the murder. You will be given clue sheets
before the play and will write down clues as you discover them. Your
clue sheet is collected before the final act, when the killer is revealed.
Maybe you will win the Super Sleuth award. The train leaves from Fort
Myers every Wednesday, Thursday, Friday, Saturday, and Sunday and
makes a 40-mile, 3.5-hour round-trip. All trains depart promptly at
6:30 p.m. (5:30 p.m. on Sundays).

9 National Naval Aviation Museum

1750 Radford Blvd., Naval Air Station Pensacola, FL 32507; 800-327-5002
navalaviationmuseum.org

US Navy pilots are among the best aviators in the world, and their
history is celebrated in this fantastic museum at Naval Air Station Pensacola. You will see more than 150 wonderfully restored airplanes and
4,000 other items related to aviation in the Navy, Marines, and Coast
Guard. You can sit in a flight simulator to get a feel for what it's like to
fly a naval aircraft, and enjoy action-packed movies in the Giant Screen
theater. The Flight Deck store has all kinds of souvenirs and mementos
related to naval aviation, and there is also a nice café. All visitors to the
National Naval Aviation Museum who do not possess a Department
of Defense identification card or are not escorted by the holder of a
such a card are required to enter and exit Naval Air Station Pensacola
through the West Gate at 1878 S. Blue Angel Pkwy.

10 Valiant Air Command Warbird Museum

Space Coast Regional Airport, 6600 Tico Road, Titusville, Florida 32780; 321-268-1941
valiantaircommand.com

This museum focuses on war planes from the earliest days of aviation
to the present day. Its collection includes nearly 50 historic warbirds.
At least nine of these planes are privately owned and in flying condition, and their owners permit the planes to be in the collection.
Among these is a replica of a Sopwith F.1 Camel, a DeHaviland DH.82
Tiger Moth, and a TBM Avenger torpedo bomber. The static collection
includes about 40 planes, including an Me 208, a MiG-15, and a F-8K
Crusader. There is also a memorabilia room with flight gear, dress
uniforms, weapons, and other artifacts.

Merritt Island National Wildlife Refuge (photographed by Steve Meese/Shutterstock)

THE RAPID DEVELOPMENT OF FLORIDA has been a double-edged sword. On the negative side, this growth has too often been rampant and careless and has done a lot of environmental damage. Native habitat has been lost forever, and what remains continues to be erased or damaged by development. On a more positive note, the financial resources generated by this growth have provided the funds for government and private organizations to buy sensitive lands for preservation. These preserves, along with nature centers and science museums, continue to educate the public about environmental issues and help them become good stewards of the land.

SCIENCE MUSEUMS AND NATURE CENTERS

1 Blowing Rocks Preserve

574 S. Beach Road, Hobe Sound, Florida 33455; 561-744-6668
tinyurl.com/blowingrocksfl

You will witness magnificent breaking waves and endangered wildlife at this environmental preserve on Jupiter Island. The limestone outcroppings here are unusual in that they are the largest outcroppings of Anastasia limestone on the East Coast. When the surf is heavy, the waves force themselves through holes in the limestone and can blow ocean spray as high as 50 feet in the air. The barrier island sanctuary harbors manatees and rare loggerhead, green, and leatherback sea turtles as well as tree species like sea grape, gumbo-limbo, and mangrove.

2 Corkscrew Swamp Sanctuary

375 Sanctuary Road W, Naples, Florida 34120; 239-348-9151
corkscrew.audubon.org

Bring your binoculars when you visit Corkscrew. In the early days of Florida's development, cypress trees were abundant in the swamps of Florida, but extensive logging operations destroyed most of them for lumber by the mid-20th century. This sanctuary has preserved the last remaining large stands of virgin bald cypress in North America. Stroll along a 2.25-mile boardwalk through pine flatwoods, wet prairies, stands of bald cypress, and learn about the wetland ecosystems. The sanctuary is a major stop on the Great Florida Birding & Wildlife Trail. The endangered wood stork and many other wetland birds breed here. Among species you might see are night herons, tricolored herons, snowy egrets, limpkins, barred owls, and swallow-tailed kites. You may also see otters, deer, turtles, and snakes. You can take a self-guided tour or enjoy one of many guided tours offered by the sanctuary staff.

3 Florida Keys Eco-Discovery Center

35 E. Quay Road, Key West, Florida 33040; 305-809-4750
floridakeys.noaa.gov/eco_discovery.html

The casual environment of this small, free nature center is just right
for laid-back Key West. The center teaches you about the native plants,
animals, and ecosystems of the Florida Keys. There are several exhibits,
including an interactive satellite map of the Florida Keys. There is also a
replica of the Aquarius Reef Base underwater ocean laboratory near Key
Largo and an underwater video camera that is used to monitor the health
of coral reefs. The Mote Marine Laboratory Living Reef exhibit contains a
2,500-gallon saltwater tank inhabited by tropical fish and living coral.

4 Gumbo Limbo Nature Center

1801 N. Ocean Blvd., Boca Raton, Florida 33432; 561-544-8605
gumbolimbo.org

This nature center packs a lot of interesting exhibits in its 20 acres
of protected barrier island. Although it has no direct Atlantic Ocean
beachfront, it has a shoreline along the Intracoastal Waterway. Its
name comes from the gumbo-limbo tree, of which there are many in
this park. There are also many other trees, such as strangler fig and
cabbage palm. The center has an indoor museum with exhibits and
aquariums, plus several outdoor aquariums displaying ecosystems for
fish, turtles, and sea life. You can enjoy a boardwalk trail and experience a small butterfly garden and a Seminole Chiki hut. Gumbo Limbo
is well known for its sea turtle rehabilitation facility, and you can see
some of the turtles under its care.

5 Harbor Branch Ocean Discovery Visitors Center

5600 N. US 1, Fort Pierce, Florida 34946; 772-242-2293
fau.edu/hboi/community/odc.php

When you step through the doors here, you will be entering Florida
Atlantic University's Harbor Branch Oceanographic Institute, a large,
functioning research facility with a storied history. Located on a 146-acre
site fronting the Indian River Lagoon north of Fort Pierce, its research
community includes approximately 200 ocean scientists, staff, and
students. Research is directed toward innovation in marine science and
engineering, conservation of coral reefs, the study of marine mammals
and fisheries, and more. The visitors center contains a video theater,
aquariums, interactive exhibits, and other displays designed to show
you the institute's exploration of the marine environment and current
research. Exhibits change frequently to reflect ongoing research and
conservation efforts. There is no charge for individuals or families.

6 Merritt Island National Wildlife Refuge

Visitor Center, 1987 Scrub Jay Way, Titusville, Florida 32782; 321-861-5601
www.fws.gov/refuge/merritt_island

It always amazes me to visit this huge refuge, nestled in the shadow of Kennedy Space Center. The space center and the refuge exist side by side on Merritt Island. The unspoiled nature of the refuge and the Space Age activity nearby make a dramatic contrast. The refuge is 140,000 acres and boasts over 1,000 species of plants and over 500 species of wildlife. It has miles of public hiking and driving trails. It is also a site on the Great Florida Birding Trail. It's best, but not mandatory, to stop first at the visitor center to get your bearings. A favorite place to see wildlife is the Black Point Wildlife Drive. This is a 7-mile drive along a dirt road through pine flatwoods and marshes. I have made this drive several times and have seen wading birds, alligators, otters, bobcats, snakes, ducks, ospreys, and eagles. You can pick up a brochure near the drive entrance that tells you what to look for. It usually takes a bit less than 1 hour to make this drive.

7 Museum of Science & Industry (MOSI)

4801 E. Fowler Ave., Tampa, Florida 33617; 813-987-6000
mosi.org

This museum is fun for people of all ages, with more than 100 hands-on activities. Among its features are a planetarium and several exhibits that explore concepts in science, health and wellness, space, and weather. Build a robot, learn about optical illusions, try to solve hands-on puzzles, explore space in a NASA-funded simulated lunar colony, and even lie on a bed of nails. Put on a pair of "drunk driving goggles" to see how alcohol affects your vision and coordination, and learn about 3-D printing and how it is changing the world. Since it's Florida, take the opportunity to experience hurricane-force winds and touch a lightning bolt. At the planetarium, a star projector can simulate the night sky at any place or time on Earth, past, present, or future.

8 | Ocala National Forest

Lake George Ranger District, 17147 E. FL 40, Silver Springs, Florida 34488; 352-625-2520
fs.usda.gov/ocala

There are many public roads that will take you into North Central Florida's Ocala National Forest. You can wander around wherever you want, but it's more fun to visit their website or stop at a visitor center to get brochures and maps to help plan your visit. The forest covers 387,000 acres and contains much of Florida's remaining sand pine scrub forest, along with more than 600 lakes, rivers, and springs. The forest is home to black bears, alligators, deer, wild boars, coyotes, foxes, possums, raccoons, otters, bobcats, skunks, armadillos, and gopher tortoises. There are numerous recreation areas, backroad trails, campgrounds, hiking trails, equestrian trails, and scenic byways. The forest also contains four wilderness areas designated by Congress as places that are totally protected from humans. Their ecosystems have completely natural environments and give adventurous people a place to test their wilderness skills, including surviving mosquitoes.

9 | Orlando Science Center

777 E. Princeton St., Orlando, Florida 32803; 407-514-2000
osc.org

With four floors of science exhibits, giant-screen movie theaters, and live programming, this science center offers many interactive experiences in the field of natural science. Get to know a real reptile or learn about the dinosaur age, physics, and gravity. Experience a flight simulator in the Flight Lab, and visit Dr. Dare's Lab to witness experiments in forensics, electricity, or chemistry. On top of the center, the Crosby Observatory has Florida's largest publicly accessible refractor telescope. This 10-inch telescope, and several smaller scopes, are available at selected times for viewing the sky, weather permitting.

10 | Wildlife Sanctuary of Northwest Florida

105 N. S St., Pensacola, Florida 32505; 850-433-9453
pensacolawildlife.com

Each year, this sanctuary provides care to more than 3,000 injured or orphaned wild animals native to Florida. When it receives an animal, the staff provide immediate medical attention and care for the animal until it can be released. Animals they have helped and released include foxes, birds, rabbits, squirrels, possums, raccoons, and skunks. Some animals that cannot be rehabilitated become permanent residents of the sanctuary. It is currently home to more than 100 of these, including bald eagles, hawks, and owls, which you can see on your visit.

A trail in Everglades National Park (photographed by Jerome Simon Dannhauer/Shutterstock)

THE FLORIDA EVERGLADES is a huge subtropical wetland of sawgrass marshes in a complex system of interdependent ecosystems. These ecosystems include cypress swamps, the estuarine mangrove forests of the Ten Thousand Islands, tropical hardwood hammocks, pine rocklands, and the saltwater marine environment of Florida Bay in the Keys. A truly massive region, the Florida Everglades sprawls across 16 counties, all the way from Orlando in the north to Monroe County in the south, and whereever you visit, it's a site to behold.

THE EVERGLADES

1 Big Cypress National Preserve

Big Cypress Swamp Welcome Center, 33000 Tamiami Trail E, Ochopee, Florida 34141; 239-695-4757
Oasis Visitor Center, 52105 Tamiami Trail E, Ochopee, Florida 34141; 239-695-4111
nps.gov/bicy

This 729,000-acre preserve was established in 1974. Unlike at adjacent Everglades National Park, the Seminole and Miccosukee Indians were given permanent rights to occupy and use portions of the land. Some live here and provide guided tours. There are two visitor centers on Tamiami Trail where you can learn about the history of the preserve and watch an informational film in which park service staffers can tell you what activities are available. The preserve is home to mangroves, orchids, alligators, snakes, birds, otters, bobcats, coyotes, black bears, and panthers. Hiking is a popular activity all year long because the trails are more walkable than those in the sawgrass prairies of the Everglades farther east. You can also arrange canoe or kayak trips, and tent, RV, and backcountry campsites are available. The preserve is an International Dark-Sky Association (IDA) Dark Sky Place. Far away from the urban development of the east and west coasts, the preserve has a night sky where you can still see thousands of stars and enjoy the Milky Way.

2 Clyde Butcher's Big Cypress Gallery

52388 Tamiami Trail, Ochopee, Florida 34141; 239-695-2428
clydebutcher.com/galleries

Photographer Clyde Butcher specializes in large-format black-and-white landscapes, especially in the Everglades. He has been called the Ansel Adams of the Everglades. A large collection of his photographs are on view in his Big Cypress Gallery, which is about 0.5 mile east of the Big Cypress National Preserve Oasis Visitor Center. The artist has other galleries in Venice and Sarasota as well.
A popular feature of this gallery is the Big Cypress Swamp Walk, conducted by Butcher himself. On this 2-hour eco-swamp tour, you will get your feet wet and see orchids, ferns, bromeliads, birds, and

many other swamp creatures. If you like, you can book a few nights at the Everglades Swamp Cottage or Bungalow, located behind the gallery. These lodgings have all the modern conveniences and tremendous views of the natural surroundings.

3 Everglades Rod and Gun Club

200 Riverside Drive, Everglades City, Florida 34139; 239-695-2101

The main reason to visit the Everglades Rod and Gun Club is to step back into history. This rambling old wooden building on the bank of the Barron River dates to the 1890s and has seen such famous guests as Ernest Hemingway and Harry Truman. I visited several times just to see the beautiful paneled lobby, bar, restaurant, and sitting rooms. The restaurant and bar operating hours seem to be ever changing, sometimes due to the season. The rooms in the main lodge are not for rent, but there are several neat and clean cabins. One word of caution: When mosquitoes decide to visit the hotel grounds, you best have plenty of insect repellent.

4 Everglades National Park

Gulf Coast Visitor Center, 815 Oyster Bar Lane, Everglades City, Florida 34139; 239-695-3311
Shark Valley Visitor Center, 36000 SW Eighth St. (US 41/Tamiami Trail), Miami, Florida 33194; 305-221-8776
Ernest F. Coe Visitor Center, 40001 FL 9336, Homestead, Florida 33034; 305-242-7700
Flamingo Visitor Center, 1 Flamingo Lodge Highway, Homestead, Florida 33034; 239-695-2945
nps.gov/ever

This national park's 1.5 million acres make it the largest tropical wilderness in the United States. It is a sensitive ecosystem of wetlands and forests in what has been called the River of Grass. This shallow, slow-moving river flows south from Lake Okeechobee toward Florida Bay. Thirty-nine threatened or endangered species can be found in the park, including the Florida panther, the West Indian manatee, 10 species of birds, 8 species of plants, 6 species of invertebrates, and 9 species of reptiles. The best time to visit is from December to March, when temperatures are cooler and mosquitoes are least active. There are four entrances at separate visitor centers. The two closest entrances to Miami are the Ernest Coe Visitor Center and the Shark Valley Visitor Center. At the Ernest Coe Visitor Center in Homestead, a 38-mile road begins, meandering through rockland, cypress, freshwater and coastal prairie, and mangroves and ending at the Flamingo Visitor Center and marina, which is open only during the busiest time of the year. I prefer the Gulf Coast entrance in Everglades City, which is closest to Naples and the west coast. This entrance provides boat tours and exhibits. It is also where canoers can access the Wilderness Waterway,

a 99-mile canoe trail that extends to the Flamingo Visitor Center. The western coast of the park and the Ten Thousand Islands are accessible only by boat.

5 Lake Okeechobee Scenic Trail

Numerous access points around the perimeter of Lake Okeechobee; 863-983-8101
www.saj.usace.army.mil/missions/civil-works/recreation/lake-okeechobee-scenic-trail

Lake Okeechobee is the largest lake in Florida and is encircled by an earthen dike that is 35 feet high and 110 miles long. The dike was built in the 1930s as a flood-control measure. Although the dike prevents a direct view of the lake from most of the roads around its shores, there is a path on its top that has been made part of the Florida National Scenic Trail. There are unobstructed views of the lake from the top of the dike. About half of the trail's length is paved and the other half is compacted gravel. The trail can be used for hiking, biking, roller blading, and horseback riding. There are 14 places along the trail that can be used for camping. There are numerous access points along the trail. Since portions of the dike are being reconstructed, the Army Corps of Engineers website continually updates which parts of the trail are available at any given time.

6 Miccosukee Indian Village

Mile marker 36, US 41 (Tamiami Trail), Miami, Florida 33194; 305-480-1924
miccosukee.com/indian-village

Most people have heard of the Seminoles, but who are the Miccosukee? They are a separate tribe with some cultural differences and they broke off from the Seminoles in 1962. In addition to a casino and gaming resort in Miami, the Miccosukee have a village farther west on the Tamiami Trail in the Everglades, about 40 miles west of Miami. Your visit will include a guided tour of the history, culture, and lifestyle of the tribe. You will see demonstrations of wood carving, beadwork, basket weaving, and doll making and learn about alligators and how the tribe has coexisted with them all these years. You can take an airboat ride into the Everglades and visit a traditional camp that has been owned by the same Miccosukee family for more than 100 years. A museum has photos of generations of tribe members, colorful native clothing, native paintings, and other tribal artifacts. The Miccosukee Restaurant serves the famous Miccosukee fry bread and pumpkin bread, plus gator, catfish, frog legs, and more.

7 Museum of the Everglades

105 Broadway Ave. W, Everglades City, Florida 34139; 239-695-0008
evergladesmuseum.org

When you visit this museum, you will enter what used to be a laundry building from the 1920s that served the Everglades Rod and Gun Club. Laundry operations ceased many years ago, and the structure is now on the National Register of Historic Places. Inside, the museum documents the history of Everglades City and the surrounding area, which was settled in the late 1800s. Early settlers survived by fishing, farming, and hunting, most making their living from the Everglades in one form or another. A recent exhibit titled "Abandoned Vehicles of the Everglades" highlighted a collection of photographs by Matt Stock that show rusty, long-abandoned vehicles that have become part of the ecosystem as the Florida jungle grows up into and through them.

8 Shark Valley Tram Tours

Shark Valley Loop Road, Miami, Florida 33194; 305-221-8455
sharkvalleytramtours.com

Shark Valley is in Everglades National Park about 40 miles west of downtown Miami. The way I have enjoyed this place in the past is with a self-guided bicycle tour using my own bike. The 15-mile paved road is an easy ride because it's flat, though it's unnerving sometimes if too many gators are napping beside the path. The ride takes 2 or 3 hours or longer depending on how often you stop. You can also rent a bicycle from Shark Valley Tram Tours. Another great way to see things is on the 2-hour Everglades Tram Tour through this section of Everglades National Park. It's a guided tour conducted by an experienced naturalist. The tour is in an open vehicle, so you get a great view of wildlife and habitat. Halfway through the tour you will come to a 45-foot-high observation platform that gives you a fantastic view of the Everglades. On a clear day you can see 20 miles in all directions. Shark Valley is busiest December 26–April 25. Reservations are highly recommended during this period.

The Everglades

9 Smallwood Store

360 Mamie St., Chokoloskee, Florida 34138; 239-695-2989
smallwoodstore.com

Smallwood Store is one of the most historic places in Southwest Florida. It is on the National Register of Historic Places. It is located on Chokoloskee Island, which is connected to Everglades City by a long causeway. The store was opened by Ted Smallwood in 1906 as a general store and trading post serving the Seminole Indians and early white settlers in the area. The building perches on stilts over the edge of the water on Chokoloskee Bay at the south end of the island. It has been opened and shut over the years, sometimes due to hurricane damage. The store is open now and still looks like what it was: an Old Florida trading post, stocking items that Ted Smallwood himself would recognize. It has no air-conditioning, but when the door is open, a nice breeze flows through. It has now survived six hurricanes, and the most recent one, Irma in 2017, took its toll. There is a fundraising campaign underway to repair and rebuild Smallwood's.

One of the many alligators of Everglades National Park (photographed by FloridaStock/Shutterstock)

Paddleboarding (photographed by goodluz/Shutterstock)

FLORIDA HAS THOUSANDS of miles of saltwater coastline, thousands of lakes, and dozens of rivers. Getting out on the water is a traditional way to enjoy the state and see sights you can't spot from the roads. Tours and adventures are readily available to help you enjoy the water, or you can rent a boat and do it on your own. Snorkeling, fishing, and sailing are activities that Floridians enjoy all year long.

ENJOYING THE WATER

1 AJ's Water Adventures

116 Harbor Blvd., Destin, Florida 32541; 850-837-2222
dolphincruisesdestinfl.com

AJ's Water Adventures covers almost everything you could want to do on the water. They give you plenty of ways to enjoy the beautiful, clear, emerald waters surrounding this Gulf Coast town. You can go on a dolphin cruise, a sunset cruise, or a leisurely sail on a 74-foot custom-built schooner named *Daniel Webster Clements*. You can also take a thrilling high-speed ride on the *Sea Quest,* a 53-foot speedboat. If you want to get into the water, they will take you on a local snorkeling trip. There are several cruise and tour packages to choose from, and every cruise comes with complimentary beer and wine (but not too much), soda, and water. They even let the kids take the helm and be captain every now and then.

2 Boggy Creek Airboat Adventures

2001 E. Southport Road, Kissimmee, Florida 34746; 407-344-9550
bcairboats.com

No visit to Florida is complete without taking an airboat ride. Moved along by engine-driven aircraft propellers, these shallow-draft craft can go into places that ordinary boats can't. Experienced captains operate Boggy Creek's fleet of 12 US Coast Guard–inspected boats, which can carry up to 17 passengers. Tours come in a variety of options, from half-hour trips to private one-hour excursions for families or groups. They even have a tour that lets you drive the airboat. The sunset and night tours are especially interesting. All of the tours will bring you up close to natural Florida wildlife, including water birds and alligators. Other attractions here include a Native American village, a simulated gem stone and fossil mine, and a tiki bar. There is also a barbecue restaurant onsite.

3 CatBoat Adventures

148 Charles Ave., Mount Dora, Florida 32757; 352-325-1442
catboattour.com

Mount Dora is a charming town on Lake Dora in the hill and lake country northwest of Orlando. One of the best ways to enjoy and explore the waters is by small boat. CatBoat Adventures provides you with a Craig Cat, a small twin-hulled boat that is powered by an outboard motor and seats two people side by side. The tour guides have their own boat and take their small fleet of visitors on a narrated tour of Lake Dora and the fascinating mile-long Dora Canal. This canal is one of the most beautiful in Florida and is like cruising through a jungle stream among 2,000-year-old cypress trees. You may see herons, egrets, ducks, ospreys, eagles, turtles, and alligators. The canal was used in 1951 to reshoot some of the river scenes from the movie *African Queen* starring Humphrey Bogart and Katharine Hepburn. The tour starts at Mount Dora Boating Center and Marina two blocks from downtown Mount Dora.

4 Florida Bay Outfitters

104050 Overseas Highway, Key Largo, Florida 33037; 305-451-3018
paddlefloridakeys.com

This operation is one of Florida's largest retailers and renters of anything related to paddle sports. Their location in the upper Keys is a great place to begin any kind of Florida Keys and South Florida paddling trip. You can buy or rent a variety of kayaks, paddleboards, and canoes, and they offer hourly or daily tours, as well as longer trips. Take a full-day tour in Everglades National Park, 7 Mile Bridge, Indian Key, or even longer two- to five-day tour of the lower Keys backcountry focusing on wildlife. You can also enjoy a full-moon tour, a paddleboard tour, a snorkel tour, and more, all led by experts. The tours are great for all levels of experience. If you want to supplement your paddling, they even have a full-day adventure on Hobie sailing kayaks among the islands of Florida Bay.

5 *Jungle Queen* Cruises

Bahia Mar Yachting Center, 801 Seabreeze Blvd., Fort Lauderdale, Florida 33316; 954-462-5596
junglequeen.com

This riverboat cruise will delight you as you glide along the many miles of waterways in Fort Lauderdale. You will learn all about the history of this great town and see the homes of many rich and famous people. The boat holds more than 500 passengers and resembles an Old Florida paddlewheel steamer from the pioneer days of Florida. The cruises take between 90 minutes and 3 hours, and some feature a buffet dinner.

6 Key West Express

1200 Main St., Fort Myers Beach, Florida 33931; 239-463-5733
100 Grinnell St., Key West, Florida 33040; 239-463-5733
951 Bald Eagle Drive, Marco Island, Florida 34145; 239-463-5733
keywestexpress.net

The Key West Express is a passenger ferry service with three vessels that operate between Fort Myers Beach, Marco Island, and Key West. It is quite often faster to visit Key West this way than to drive. The fleet consists of the 155-foot *Big Cat Express,* the 134-foot *AtlantiCat*, and the 170-foot *Key West Express*. Each of these twin-hulled craft has a cruising speed of more than 30 knots (about 40 miles per hour). That's faster than the destroyer I served on in the Navy. Both vessels have air-conditioned interiors, several sun decks, a full-service galley and bar, satellite television, and plenty of places to sit and relax. Each boat is fully certified by the US Coast Guard. Travel times between Key West and the other ports (and vice versa) are usually about 3.5 hours, depending on the weather. Boarding time from Fort Myers Beach and Marco Island is usually 7 a.m. From Key West, boarding begins at either 4 or 5 p.m. You can also depart and return on different days.

7 *Naples Princess* Cruises

550 Port O Call Way, Naples, Florida 34102; 239-649-2275
naplesprincesscruises.com

The *Naples Princess* is a 105-foot luxury yacht approved by the Coast Guard for up to 149 passengers. It is quite often used for private charters and parties, but also offers daily public cruises. The yacht has a beautiful cherry-wood interior and gold-plated reflective ceilings. It's a wonderful place to view the historical landmarks and luxury mansions of Naples, and some wildlife as well. The daily public cruises begin from the docks at Port of Naples Marina across from Tin City near downtown Naples. The yacht cruises leisurely down Naples Bay to view the magnificent homes in Port Royal, then out Gordon Pass to the Gulf of Mexico. If you are on the sunset tour, this

Enjoying
the Water

is where you will watch one of the famous Gulf sunsets. You are likely to see dolphins and seabirds on your trip. The yacht has two full-service cash bars.

8 River Safaris

10823 W. Yulee Drive, Homosassa, Florida 34448; 352-628-5222
riversafaris.com

River Safaris is in Old Homosassa on a waterway that leads to the Homosassa River and passes Monkey Island. You can spend a day in Homosassa, basing your adventures from here. They have rental boats, airboat tours, boat rentals, pontoon boat tours, manatee tours, scalloping and fishing adventures, a gift shop with local art, three alligators who live in a pen onsite, and more. Try the 2-hour twilight dolphin watching and tiki bar pontoon tour.

9 Scenic Boat Tour

312 E. Morse Blvd., Winter Park, Florida 32789; 407-644-4056
scenicboattours.com

The Winter Park Scenic Boat Tour has been entertaining visitors since 1938. It is only an hour-long ride, but you will have plenty of fun during that hour. The pontoon boats cruise on a route between Lakes Osceola, Virginia, and Maitland, passing some of the most expensive real estate in Florida. You will see many tropical trees and plants along the route, especially in the canals that connect the lakes. You will also learn about the famous structures in Winter Park history and who lived there then and who lives there now. The tour guides are local captains who know the lake area well and keep you interested from beginning to end.

10 The Schooner Freedom

111 Avenida Menendez, St. Augustine, Florida 32084; 904-810-1010
schoonerfreedom.com

I love to sail, and this is an easy way to do it. Enjoy seeing the sights of St. Augustine and learn about its fascinating history aboard *The Schooner Freedom,* a 76-foot gaff-rigged topsail vessel that is well known around these waters. Captain John Zaruba and his wife, Admiral Sarah, have been sailing the schooner in St. Augustine since 2001. You can pitch in and help sail the boat, or just relax and enjoy a complimentary drink. If the weather is OK, John and Sarah might even let you take the helm. There is plenty of protected water around St. Augustine, and the schooner goes wherever the wind takes it. You will typically see some dolphins on the trip, as well as seabirds and other wildlife. They offer day sails, sunset sails, and moonlight sails. The day sails take about 2 hours.

11 St. Johns Rivership Co.

433 N. Palmetto Ave., Sanford, Florida 32771; 321-441-3030
stjohnsrivershipco.com

Any journey on the north-flowing St. Johns River is a trip into Florida history. This river has been a major transportation route for centuries, and many of the state's oldest towns are along its shores, yet it still has miles of pristine undeveloped shoreline. The St. Johns Rivership Co. offers a comfortable way to enjoy the river on the *Barbara-Lee,* a 105-foot modern ship built to resemble the stern-wheelers of old. The five-deck vessel features ornate wrought iron railings and massive wooden paddle wheels and can handle 194 passengers. *Barbara-Lee* departs from downtown Sanford almost every day. Several types of cruises are offered, and all narrated cruises provide you with a well-stocked bar and an entrée prepared by a professional chef. You will cruise along the river enjoying the view of wildlife and lush vegetation in air-conditioned comfort while enjoying live musical entertainment.

12 Water Taxi

10 boarding locations in Fort Lauderdale; 954-467-6677
watertaxi.com

The water taxi is an enjoyable way to visit and explore the Fort Lauderdale area. You can enjoy your trip as an individual, a family, or a group (by reservation). As you cruise along the waterways, your captain will point out mansions of famous people and landmarks and fill you in on the history of the area you are visiting. You will see hundreds of mega yachts, as Fort Lauderdale is the yachting capital of the world. Buy an all-day pass to board a vessel at any one of 10 locations and ride the taxi all day (find a map of the locations on the website). You can also buy happy hour and monthly passes. It is good manners to leave your crew members a tip.

An Everglades airboat (photographed by Stanislaw Bozek/Shutterstock)

FL 0599 MJ

At the Silver Spurs Rodeo (photographed by rusty_clark/9651437262/flickr.com/)

FLORIDA FESTIVALS CELEBRATE the art, music, and culture of the state. With a population of more than 21 million and a geographic and cultural diversity unlike any other state, there is always something going on that you will enjoy, whether it's art, music, sports, or simply the people-watching. Some events celebrate Southern culture, especially in north and central Florida. Other activities feature Latin or African-American music, art, and culture. Whatever your interests, you can find it at one of our festivals.

FESTIVALS

1 Calle Ocho Music Festival

Calle Ocho, between SW 12th Avenue and SW 27th Avenue, Miami, Florida; 305-644-8888 (Kiwanis Club of Little Havana)
carnavalmiami.com/events/calle-ocho

I think I have been part of only one world record in my life. The Calle Ocho Music Festival is in the *Guinness World Records* book for the longest conga line in the world—119,986 people in March 1988—and I was in the line. The festival celebrates Latin culture and music every March for one week. The final event on Sunday is one of the largest street festivals or block parties in the world. On this day, about 15 blocks of the Little Havana neighborhood are blocked off to traffic and opened to people. The streets are jammed with Latin music and performers, and hundreds of food booths serve just about every Latin dish you can imagine. You will hear merengue, tango, salsa, reggae, and other Caribbean and South American music. Kings or queens of the festival in the past have included Desi Arnaz, Willy Chirino, Gloria Estefan, and many other star performers.

2 Fiesta of Five Flags

2121 W. Intendencia St., Pensacola, Florida 32502; 850-433-6512
fiestapensacola.org

Pensacola is known as the City of Five Flags. It was founded in 1559 by Spanish Conquistador Don Tristan de Luna and was the first European settlement in the United States. Since then, the flags of four more nations have flown over Pensacola: French, British, Confederate, and American. Although Pensacola is older than St. Augustine, St. Augustine claims the title of oldest *continuously occupied* city in the United States. This technicality doesn't dampen Pensacola's enthusiasm for its own history and heritage; rather, the Fiesta of Five Flags celebrates this heritage. Since 1950, it has been held the first two weeks in June and lasts 10 days. The festival kicks off in Seville Quarter, the historic district of Pensacola, and opening day features live music, food, flags, and decorations celebrating the

Festivals

diverse heritage of the city. You will see many parades, music performances, art and sculpture contests, and the de Luna Landing Ceremony. People enjoy the festivities both from land and boats.

3 Florida Folk Festival

Stephen Foster Folk Culture Center State Park, 11016 Lillian Saunders Drive, White Springs, Florida 32096; 386-397-4331
floridastateparks.org/floridafolkfestival

If you love Florida history and music, the Florida Folk Festival is a must see. It takes place every Memorial Day weekend at Stephen Foster Folk Culture Center State Park on the Suwannee River near White Springs. You will see exhibits showing how Florida pioneers lived and survived in the harsh environment that existed in the days before mosquito control and air-conditioning. At the three-day event, you will hear storytellers, well-known Florida musicians, fiddle tunes, and other music brought to Florida by many generations of immigrants that have made the state their home. There are usually about 300 musical performances over the three-day weekend. Hundreds of vendors and artists have their Florida-themed wares on display, and good food is for sale all around the park, including collard greens, cornbread, chicken perlo, shrimp gumbo, and hoppin' John. The state park itself is also an attraction, offering 45 campsites and other amenities. If you want to spend the weekend in the area, you can find more campgrounds and motels in nearby White Springs, Lake City, Jasper, Jennings, and Live Oak.

4 Gasparilla Pirate Festival

Tampa Bay and downtown Tampa
gasparillapiratefest.com

Celebrated every year since 1904, this festival usually takes place in late January or early February. Its highlight is an "invasion" of downtown Tampa by a 165-foot "pirate ship" named *Jose Gasparilla* and its motley crew of pirates. Tampa Bay and the Hillsborough River turn into a floating armada of pirates and citizens having a great old time. The event celebrates José Gaspar, the legendary pirate who is said to have roamed the waters of southwest Florida. Gaspar was probably fictional, but the celebrants of this festival don't care one way or the other. The festival is a Tampa institution with deep cultural and historical roots. When the ship reaches Tampa, the mayor presents the key to the city to the captain of Ye Mystic Krewe of Gasparilla, an old organization that many Tampans are proud to belong to and that has sponsored the festival for years. Some of the members descend from the crew that held the first festival in 1904. This presentation is followed by a parade with marching bands and drill teams on Bayshore Boulevard.

Festivals

5 Mug Race

133 Crystal Cove Drive, Palatka, Florida 32177; 904-264-4094 (Rudder Club of Jacksonville)
www.rudderclub.com/mug.html

This is an unusual race you can participate in or enjoy watching. Billed as the world's longest river race for sailboats, the Mug Race starts in Palatka at 7 a.m. on the first Saturday of May and runs north for 35 nautical miles on the St. Johns River to the Buckman Bridge in Orange Park. Boats are divided into classes, and no boat can have a mast higher than 44 feet because of the clearance of one of the bridges along the route. Multihull boats start first, followed by monohull ones. Boats cannot use their engines. The fastest any boat has ever made the trip is just under 3 hours, but typical times are much longer, sometimes 12 hours or more depending on the wind and stamina of the sailors. Some boats don't finish. This is Florida; some days are windy, some are not. If you have a boat with an outboard motor, it's fun to watch the race from the water. There are also vantage points along the banks of the St. Johns River where you can watch the fleet go by. The first Mug Race was in 1954. It is sponsored by the Rudder Club of Jacksonville.

6 Silver Spurs Rodeo

Osceola Heritage Park/Silver Spurs Arena, 1875 Silver Spur Lane, Kissimmee, Florida 34744; 321-697-3495
silverspursrodeo.com

You will be close to the action during this historic rodeo, the largest east of the Mississippi River. It's fun to attend both for the exciting entertainment and the link to Florida history. The original Silver Spurs rodeo started in 1944, when the Florida Cracker culture was strong, cattle was king, and the ranches needed lots of cowboys to work the business. This rodeo is a celebration of those Old Florida days. You will see bull riding, bronco busting, barrel racing, calf roping, and other events. The rodeo is held on the third weekend in February in the Silver Spurs Arena, part of the 150-acre Osceola Heritage Park on US 192 east of Kissimmee. The arena seats more than 11,000.

7 SunFest

Flagler Drive from Banyan Boulevard to Lakeview Avenue, West Palm Beach;
561-659-5980
sunfest.com

You will want to be a part of Florida's largest waterfront music and art festival. Every year more than 130,000 people crowd into downtown West Palm Beach for the event, which takes place Thursday–Sunday of the first week in May on Flagler Drive along the Intracoastal Waterway, in the West Palm Beach Arts and Entertainment District. Musical groups that have performed in the past include Keith Urban, the B-52s, Gregg Allman, Earth Wind & Fire, the Preservation Hall Jazz Band, Hootie and the Blowfish, and Ziggy Marley. Arts and crafts from more than 80 vendors are also displayed. Exhibits include jewelry, painting, pottery, ceramics, photography, sculpture, and wood. The grand finale of the weekend is a fireworks show on Sunday evening.

8 Winterfest Boat Parade

Corporate Headquarters, 512 NE Third Ave., Fort Lauderdale, Florida 33301;
954-767-0686
winterfestparade.com

I never get tired of the Winterfest Boat Parade, an annual event held every December in Fort Lauderdale. All kinds of boats, from those just 20 feet long to huge mega yachts, dress up in lights and decorations and cruise along the New River and Intracoastal Waterway. The parade begins at 6:30 p.m. when all the boats gather along the New River downtown. The parade route runs a total of 12 miles to Pompano Beach. The extravagantly lighted vessels quite often also have musical groups aboard. One way to watch the parade is to wrangle a ride on one of the parade boats, or find a friend with a boat who is willing to follow the parade. There are also plenty of spots along the river and waterway to watch, but get there early. Several waterfront restaurants and bars along the route have seating with a view, and this is my favorite way to watch, comfortably seated in a friendly watering hole (you can find a list of waterfront restaurants on the above website). Make reservations weeks in advance, however. There is also a grandstand viewing area inside Hugh Taylor Birch State Park north of Sunrise Boulevard.

Festivals

9 Worm Gruntin' Festival

Town center, 1 block off US 319, Sopchoppy, Florida 32358; wormgruntinfestival.com

Old-timers may remember Charles Kuralt of the *CBS Sunday Morning* show. Back in 1972, he participated in worm grunting in Sopchoppy, a tiny town about 33 miles south of Tallahassee, and I watched it on TV. In later years Mike Rowe featured it on his show *Dirty Jobs*. Sopchoppy has held the annual Worm Gruntin' Festival to showcase their skills since 2000. Worm gruntin' (Sopchoppy folks leave off the *g*) is a technique for drawing worms out of the ground so they can be scooped up and used for fish bait. It involves driving a wooden stake into the ground and rubbing it with a piece of iron to make it vibrate. This makes worms crawl up to the surface because they think the sound is made by moles digging (their natural predator). Some folks use a hand saw; others prefer an old leaf spring from a car. You and your kids can participate if you'd like. The event, held on the second Saturday in April, also has arts and crafts vendors and food booths to keep you busy, and live music will keep your toes tapping. Admission is free.

The festival in Sopchoppy is all about calling the most earthworms (photographed by sivivolk/Shutterstock)

Florida Caverns State Park, Marianna (photographed by IrinaK/Shutterstock)

FLORIDA PARKS ARE TREASURED natural resources. The Old Florida that is rapidly disappearing from the state is being preserved in local, state, and national parks. It is because of these parks that some parts of natural Florida are still alive and well despite the proliferation of condos, theme parks, subdivisions and shopping malls that have obliterated much of the Florida landscape in the past half century or so. Many state parks have campsites carved out of the surrounding pinewoods and palmettos. This natural vegetation gives the sites much greater privacy than you might find in the average private campground.

PARKS

1 Biscayne National Park

9700 SW 328th St., Sir Lancelot Jones Way, Homestead, Florida 33033;
305-230-1144
nps.gov/bisc

I have enjoyed sailing in Biscayne Bay more than anywhere else in Florida. Even though it is in the heart of Miami and the rest of urbanized South Florida, it has some of the clearest waters in the state. This is because much of the bay is within Biscayne National Park. The park is nearly 173,000 acres and is 95 percent underwater. It's a thrill to be boating within sight of the massive skyscrapers of downtown Miami while still feeling worlds away. If you love the outdoors, you will enjoy yourself in this park. You can snorkel, camp, boat, watch wildlife, fish, take guided eco-adventures, or just relax. Several private concessions offer full-day tours in the park that include snorkeling, hiking, paddling, and sailing. Mainland access to the park is from park headquarters at Convoy Point. Local parks and marinas also provide access. The park protects Stiltsville, once a community of 27 houses perched on stilts. Only a few buildings survived Hurricane Andrew in 1992, and they are all unoccupied. The park has a few mooring buoys near Fowey Rocks lighthouse for private boaters. Personal watercraft such as Jet Skis are prohibited.

2 Devil's Millhopper Geological State Park

4732 Millhopper Road, Gainesville, Florida 32653; 352-955-2008
floridastateparks.org/parks-and-trails/devils-millhopper-geological-state-park

I have lived in Florida most of my life, and this park is unlike the rest of the state. It will give you the feeling of being in another world. You walk down a 232-step wooden staircase into the bottom of a geological formation that has been attracting visitors for well over a century—a sinkhole that is 120 feet deep and has a diameter of 500 feet. The geology here has created a miniature rain forest in the middle of North Central Florida. You will see gentle streams of clear water trickling down the limestone walls. These miniature waterfalls and the coolness of the place make it a refreshing escape from the busy Florida environment that surrounds it. Sometimes volunteer guides are on duty and will give you inside stories about the park.

3 Dry Tortugas National Park

40001 FL 9336, Homestead, Florida 33034; 305-242-7700
nps.gov/drto

You can take a long day trip or enjoy a camping adventure by visiting Dry Tortugas National Park about 70 miles west of Key West. This 100-square-mile park is made up of seven small islands and is accessible only by boat or seaplane. The park is famous for its centerpiece attraction, the imposing Fort Jefferson, the place where Dr. Mudd was imprisoned for treating John Wilkes Booth's broken leg after President Lincoln's assassination. The islands are surrounded by clear blue waters, beautiful coral reefs teeming with marine life, and a large bird population. There are several popular ways to make the trip to the park. You can bring your own boat, charter a boat or seaplane in Key West, or take a passenger ferry. The way I prefer is to take the *Yankee Freedom III*, a high-speed catamaran ferry that takes about 2 hours and 10 minutes. It stays at the park for about 4 hours, giving you plenty of time to explore.

4 Florida Caverns State Park

3345 Caverns Road, Marianna, Florida 32446; 850-482-1228
floridastateparks.org/parks-and-trails/florida-caverns-state-park

This is another natural attraction that will make you feel like you are not in Florida. It is your chance to explore a network of underground caves created from limestone formations that have slowly dissolved over thousands of years. You will enjoy the cool air, the drip-drip-drip of trickling water, and breathtaking views of mysterious stalactites and stalagmites. You will move from cave to cave and see the many chisel marks made in the 1930s by Civilian Conservation Corps workers, who enlarged the cave passageways by hand so visitors could stand upright during guided tours. These workers also built the park's spacious visitor center. Prior to Hurricane Michael in 2018, the park also offered multiuse trails, camping, boating, and fishing; however, due to damage sustained in the hurricane, only the ranger station, visitor center, museum, and cave tours are currently open. Please check the website for the latest updates.

5 Fruit & Spice Park

24801 SW 187th Ave., Homestead, Florida 33031; 305-247-5727
redlandfruitandspice.com

Fruit & Spice Park is one of the most unusual parks in Florida. It was an eye-opener to me when I realized that fruit and spices could be so much fun. The park is in the heart of an agricultural wonder called the Redland, named for the dominant red clay soil. Plants grow in the Redland that won't grow elsewhere in Florida or America, including species native to tropical areas of Asia or South America. More than 500 varieties of exotic fruits, vegetables, herbs, spices, and nuts from all over the world are found in the 37-acre Fruit & Spice Park, established in 1944 and operated by Miami-Dade County. Its collection includes specimens from the Americas, Africa, Australia and the Pacific, Asia, and the Mediterranean, including 180 varieties of mangos, 70 varieties of bamboo, 40 varieties of bananas, and 15 varieties of jackfruit trees. The park has a nice little café serving salads, sandwiches, wraps, and pizza. The friendly staff will let you sample some of the garden delights from a serving platter they keep on hand. Guided tours of the park are conducted daily at 11 a.m, 1:30 p.m, and 3 p.m.

6 Highlands Hammock State Park

5931 Hammock Road, Sebring, Florida 33872; 863-386-6094
floridastateparks.org/parks-and-trails/highlands-hammock-state-park

I love driving through this beautiful park. If I have more time, I take a tram ride and let somebody else do the driving. You can also hike on its nine trails or ride your bike on a 3-mile loop trail. Open since 1931, it's one of the oldest state parks and has more than 9,000 acres that encompass a thriving ecosystem. Highlands Hammock has one of Florida's most diverse collections of plant and animal life, with 1,000-year-old oaks, old-growth hammock, and Florida panthers. Ferns and air plants are almost everywhere you look. You might even see a black bear. An elevated boardwalk crosses a cypress swamp, and from here you may see alligators, birds, and other wildlife. Picnicking, bird-watching, and ranger-guided tours are other popular activities. The tram tour gives you the opportunity to view wildlife relatively close-up, in areas of the park that are restricted to public access. Highlands Hammock also provides a full-facility campground.

7 Marjorie Kinnan Rawlings Historic State Park

18700 S. County Road 325, Cross Creek, Florida 32640; 352-466-3672
floridastateparks.org/parks-and-trails/marjorie-kinnan-rawlings-historic-state-park

Marjorie Kinnan Rawlings won the Pulitzer Prize for her novel *The Yearling*. She also wrote a book titled *Cross Creek* about her years living here. She wrote both books here in her little house, and you will see her old typewriter and feel like she might pop back into the room at any minute. Her Florida Cracker–style home and farm have been preserved and restored, allowing visitors to experience what 1930s farm life was like when she lived and worked here. The park is open daily, and rangers in period costume lead tours of the house October–July, Thursday–Sunday at 10 and 11 a.m. and at 1, 2, 3, and 4 p.m. You can also explore Rawlings's farmyard, grove, seasonal garden, and trails. An adjacent county park has picnic facilities, a boat ramp to Orange Lake, and a playground.

Sunset at Mallory Square (photographed by Ricardo Reitmeyer/Shutterstock)

THE FLORIDA KEYS are a string of coral cays that stretch from the mainland south of Miami all the way through Key West to the Dry Tortugas. Instead of sand beaches, most of these cays have shores of coral rock. The Keys are known for their unique geology, a fascinating culture, and a sometimes turbulent history. In 1982 the people of Key West had a disagreement with the US government, and jokingly declared their independence, briefly becoming the Conch Republic. This brought much publicity to The Keys and cemented its quirky reputation. The image still sticks today. The Keys are for people who love boating, fishing, and the unusual.

THE KEYS

1, 2, 3, 4, 5

1 Bahia Honda State Park

36850 Overseas Highway, Big Pine Key, Florida 33043; 305-872-2353
floridastateparks.org/parks-and-trails/bahia-honda-state-park

About 30 miles before you get to Key West on the Overseas Highway, you will come to Bahia Honda State Park and want to stop and linger for a few hours or a few days. The address says Big Pine Key, but the park is located on Bahia Honda Key, a largely undeveloped key with its original natural setting. This beautiful park gives you open views of the ocean from the historic Old Bahia Honda Bridge. Other activities include swimming, boating, fishing, and snorkeling. The beautiful sandy beaches here are unusual in the coral-rimmed Keys, and the views of the sunset are amazing. The park's campground is one of the most popular in the state. You can make campsite reservations 11 months in advance, and many people do. Bahia Honda is an excellent place to see wading birds and shorebirds, while the Sand and Sea Nature Center introduces nature lovers to the island's plants and animals.

2 Dolphin Connection

61 Hawks Cay Blvd., Duck Key, Florida 33050; 305-289-0136
dolphinconnection.com

Dolphin Connection has been in business since 1990 and is located at the Hawks Cay Resort. As the name implies, they focus on dolphins and have a worldwide reputation as experts on the bottlenose dolphin. The facility is centered around a circular saltwater lagoon. You will be able to meet dolphins and will be amazed at the obvious intelligence and natural good nature of these friendly mammals. The owners and employees of this facility believe in providing the highest possible care to their dolphins. There are various levels of experiences available, ranging from interacting with the dolphins from a dock to getting in the water with them to the 3-hour Trainer-for-a-Day program.

3 The Ernest Hemingway Home & Museum

907 Whitehead St., Key West, Florida 33040; 305-294-1136
hemingwayhome.com

In 1931 Key West became the home of Ernest and Pauline Hemingway. Built in 1851 in the Spanish Colonial style, the home was constructed using limestone excavated at the home site. The resulting pit created a large basement, rare in the Keys. Another rarity was the swimming pool that Hemingway built for what would be about $360,000 in today's dollars. Ernest kidded his wife about the cost of the pool, saying, "Pauline, you've spent all but my last penny, so you might as well have that!" Visitors can see that penny embedded in the stones by the pool. You will probably also see some polydactyl (six-toed) cats on the property. These are the beloved and well-cared-for descendants of a polydactyl cat given to Hemingway by a visiting sea captain. The home's interior is filled with European antiques and animal trophies from Hemingway's African safaris.

4 Key West Aquarium

1 Whitehead St., Key West, Florida 33040; 888-544-5927
keywestaquarium.com

The Key West Aquarium was built by the federal government's Works Progress Administration from 1933 to 1935. It was then the world's only open-air aquarium. This is a simple aquarium without a lot of the high-tech adventures typical in many modern big-city establishments. One of the goals of the aquarium is to help preserve the natural habitat and animals of the Florida Keys. Contributing to that effort is the sea turtle conservation program, where injured sea turtles are rehabilitated and released. In addition to exhibits devoted to alligators, sharks, jellyfish, and sting rays, you will also see many game and reef fish such as cobia, tarpon, angelfish, and parrotfish.

5 Mallory Square

400 Wall S., Key West, Florida 33040; 305-809-3700
mallorysquare.com

From the earliest visits I made to Key West many years ago until now, the public area of Mallory Square has been the gathering place for locals and tourists to enjoy the sunset and entertainment. The square is located near the north end of Duval Street and fronts the Gulf of Mexico. Its Sunset Celebration includes arts and craft shows, street performers, and food carts. The sunset is still the main attraction, but you can also dine in one of the restaurants or shop in a retail outlet. One of the sights to see in Mallory Square is the Key West Historic Memorial Sculpture Garden, which contains bronze busts of people who had a

major impact on the history of Key West. Joining the busts of many local home-grown heroes are those of Henry Flagler, Ernest Hemingway, Harry S. Truman, and permanent and part-time residents.

6 Theater of the Sea

84721 Overseas Highway, Islamorada, Florida 33036; 305-664-2431
theaterofthesea.com

Theater of the Sea is a family-owned venture that has been in business since 1946. It is one of the oldest marine facilities in the world. The lagoons and tropical gardens are home to dolphins, sea lions, sea turtles, tropical fish, game fish, sharks, stingrays, alligators, birds, and others. You will get to observe various shows from up close involving dolphins, sea lions, parrots, and other animals. There are also many interactive programs such as swimming with a sea lion or a dolphin. You can get close for a view of sea turtles and even alligators. Attractions include a bottomless boat ride, a fish and reptile tour, walking on a lagoon beach, and much more. The dolphin swims are 30 minutes and include dorsal tows, hugs, and swimming and snorkeling.

7 Harry S. Truman Little White House

111 Front St., Key West, Florida 33040; 305-294-9911
trumanlittlewhitehouse.com

This old home in the Truman Annex neighborhood is Florida's only presidential museum. Harry S. Truman, the 33rd president of the United States, loved Key West and made this house his winter White House. The home is filled with the original furniture, documents, and memorabilia from Truman's time, and guides and video presentations will tell you all about those years and before. President Truman stayed here for a total of 175 days during his presidential term, but before that, the house served as the naval station's command headquarters during the Spanish-American War and World Wars I and II. Other famous residents include inventor Thomas Edison, who lived here during World War I while working on underwater weapons. The house is still used for government functions today.

Harry Truman's Little White House in Key West, Florida
(photographed by Deantonphotos/Shutterstock)

Florida is a hotspot for baseball fans (photographed by zimmytws/shutterstock)

BOASTING TWO MAJOR LEAGUE BASEBALL TEAMS, three NFL football teams, two NBA basketball teams, a professional soccer club, a pair of NHL teams, and some of the best collegiate teams in the country, Florida is a sports fan's dream. And thanks to its mild winters, it's also the home of Major League Baseball's spring training, beckoning baseball fans from all over. If that's not enough, it also is home to plenty of minor league and semi-professional teams that are more than worth watching.

SPORTS

Baseball

Miami Marlins
Marlins Park, 501 Marlins Way, Miami, Florida 33125; 305-480-1300
mlb.com/marlins

Tampa Bay Rays
Tropicana Field, 1 Tropicana Field Drive, St. Petersburg, Florida 33705; 888-326-7297
mlb.com/rays

Basketball

Miami Heat
American Airlines Arena, 601 Biscayne Blvd., Miami, Florida 33132; 786-777-1000
nba.com/heat/home

Orlando Magic
Amway Center, 400 W. Church St., Orlando, Florida 32801; 407-896-2442
nba.com/magic

Football

Jacksonville Jaguars
TIAA Bank Field, 1 TIAA Bank Field Drive, Jacksonville, Florida 32202; 904-633-2000
jaguars.com

Miami Dolphins
Hard Rock Stadium, 347 Don Shula Drive, Miami Gardens, Florida 33056; 305-943-8000
miamidolphins.com

Tampa Bay Buccaneers
Raymond James Stadium, 4201 N. Dale Mabry Highway, Tampa, Florida 33607;
813-870-2700
buccaneers.com

Hockey

Florida Panthers
BB&T Center, 1 Panther Pkwy., Sunrise, Florida 33323; 954-835-7000
nhl.com/panthers

Tampa Bay Lightning
Amalie Arena, 401 Channelside Drive, Tampa, Florida 33602; 813-301-6500
nhl.com/lightning

Lacrosse

Florida Launch
Central Broward Stadium, 3700 NW 11th Place, Lauderhill, Florida 33311;
561-923-9067
floridalaunchlacrosse.com

Soccer

Orlando City Soccer Club
Orlando City Stadium, 655 W. Church St., Orlando, Florida 32805; 855-675-2489
orlandocitysc.com

Miscellaneous

50 Florida Minor League and Semi-Pro Teams in All Sports
en.wikipedia.org/wiki/Sports_teams_in_Florida#Minor_league_and_semi-pro_teams

Guide to Florida Spring Training Sites for Major League Baseball Teams
floridagrapefruitleague.com/home/freeguide

51 Florida NCAA Division 1 Teams
fieldlevel.com.explore-teams/all/fl/ncaad1

INDEX

All locations are in Florida unless otherwise specified. Page references in italics indicate photos from accounts in the book.

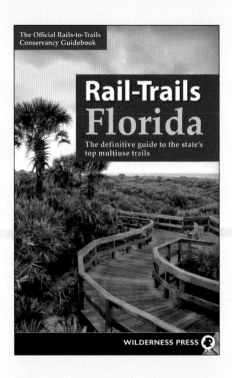

Check out this great title from **WILDERNESS PRESS!**

Rail-Trails Florida

Rails-to-Trails Conservancy

ISBN: 978-0-89997-819-2 • $16.95 • 5.5 x 8.5 • paperback
192 pages • full color • maps and photos

The Official Rails-to-Trails Conservancy Guidebook

Explore 52 of the best rail-trails and multiuse pathways across Florida. You'll appreciate the detailed maps for each trail, plus driving directions to trailheads. Quick, at-a-glance icons indicate which activities each trail can accommodate, from biking to fishing to horseback riding. The succinct descriptions are written by rail-trail experts, so you know it's information that you can rely on!

"Excellent descriptions and logistical help." —*Canoe & Kayak*

CANOEING & KAYAKING
FLORIDA
3RD EDITION

Johnny Molloy

MENASHA RIDGE PRESS
Your Guide to the Outdoors Since 1982

Check out this great title from ***MENASHA RIDGE PRESS!***

Canoeing & Kayaking Florida

Johnny Molloy

**ISBN: 978-1-63404-030-3 • $18.95 • 3rd edition
6 x 9 • paperback • 336 pages • maps and photos**

Wet Your Paddle and Whet Your Taste for Adventure

Explore hidden Florida with the most comprehensive guide to unique streams, springs, creeks, and rivers. Perfect for novice and experienced paddlers alike, this edition features details on nearly 100 top paddling trips—complete with maps, river profiles, ratings for solitude and scenery, and more! For over 30 years, *Canoeing & Kayaking Florida* has provided the essential information needed to paddle the state's waterways. Let it be your guide to the Sunshine State.

About the Author

Mike Miller is a blogger, writer, consulting engineer, and speaker who has lived in Florida most of his life. He owns the popular website FloridaBackroadsTravel.com and is the author of 18 books about Florida. His writing focuses on Florida off-the-beaten path and tells readers about the rich Florida history that informs their travel. He has driven an estimated 2 million miles in Florida in too many cars to count and has sailed all of Florida coasts and Keys in sailboats.

Mike received a B.S. in Civil Engineering from the University of Florida and is a registered professional engineer and licensed real estate broker. He served in the U.S. Navy, owned his own consulting engineering firm, and had key roles in the construction of Walt Disney World, Epcot, and Universal Studios Florida. He loves to write and speak about Florida.

Florida Day Trips celebrates Florida's unique nature and reflects Mike's lifetime of exploring the Sunshine State.